DATE DUE			
DE 3 '78			

THE
FAMILY

YESTERDAY

TODAY

TOMORROW

BY WALTER GOODMAN

The Clowns of Commerce / *All Honorable Men*

The Committee / *Black Bondage*

A Percentage of the Take

BY ELAINE AND WALTER GOODMAN

The Rights of the People

THE
FAMILY

YESTERDAY

TODAY

TOMORROW

Elaine and Walter Goodman

FARRAR, STRAUS AND GIROUX

NEW YORK

Library of Congress Cataloging in Publication Data
Goodman, Elaine. / The family: yesterday, today, tomorrow.
Bibliography: p. 107 / Includes index.
1. Family—History—Juvenile literature. [1. Family]
I. Goodman, Walter, joint author. II. Title.
HQ503.G62 1975 / 301.42'09 / 74–32069
ISBN 0–374–32260–0

To our family

nuclear and extended

Especially

Sadie Goodman / Hyman Goodman

Dorothy Egan / Abe Egan / Hal Goodman

Bennet Goodman / Fran Wilder / Les Wilder

Sandy Wilder / Bonnie Wilder / Betty Hudes

Irving Hudes / Bettye Goodman / Danny Goodman

Mickey Goodman / Laurie Goodman / Robin Gulden

Danny Gulden

We are grateful to Professor Solomon Miller, chairman

of the Anthropology Department at Hofstra University,

who was kind enough to read the chapters on the primitive

family and warn us of where we were going astray.

CONTENTS

In the beginning, when Tvashtri came to the creation of woman, he found that he had exhausted his materials in the making of man and that no solid elements were left. In this dilemma, after profound meditation, he did as follows. He took the rotundity of the moon, and the curves of creepers, and the clinging of tendrils, and the trembling of grass, and the slenderness of the reed, and the bloom of flowers, and the lightness of leaves, and the tapering of the elephant's trunk, and the glances of deer, and the clustering of rows of bees, and the joyous gaiety of sunbeams, and the weeping of clouds, and the fickleness of the winds, and the timidity of the hare, and the vanity of the peacock, and the softness of the parrot's bosom, and the hardness of adamant, and the sweetness of honey, and the cruelty of the tiger, and the warm glow of fire, and the coldness of snow, and the chattering of jays, and the cooing of the kokila, *and the hypocrisy of the crane, and the fidelity of the* chakrawaka, *and compounding all these together, he made woman and gave her to man.*

But, after one week, man came to him and said, "Lord, this creature that you have given me makes my life miserable. She chatters incessantly and teases me beyond endurance, never leaving me alone; and she requires constant attention, and takes up all my time, and cries about nothing, and is always idle; and so I have come to give her back, as I cannot live with her."

So Tvashtri said, "Very well." And he took her back.

Then, after another week, man came again to him and said, "Lord, I find that my life is very lonely since I gave you back that creature. I remember how she used to dance and sing for me, and look at me out of the corner of her eye, and play with me, and cling to me; and her laughter was music, and she was beautiful to look at, and soft to touch. So give her back to me."

So Tvashtri said, "Very well." And he gave her back.

Then, after only three days, man came to him again and said, "Lord, I know not how it is; but, after all, I have come to the conclusion that she is more trouble than pleasure to me. So please take her back again."

But Tvashtri said, "Out on you. Be off. I will have no more of this. You must manage how you can."

Then man said, "But I cannot live with her."

And Tvashtri replied, "Neither could you live without her." And he turned his back on man, and went on with his work.

Then man said, "What is to be done? For I cannot live either with her or without her."

A S A N S K R I T   M Y T H

THE

FAMILY

———

YESTERDAY

TODAY

TOMORROW

FOREWORD

The Family under Attack

The family as most Americans know it and as it exists throughout the Western world—husband, wife, and two or three children more or less—has lately come under attack. It is charged, among other things, with being narrow, restrictive, confining, emotionally suffocating both for parents and for children, and bad for the whole society. Its critics argue that the typical American family narrows the individual's range of human relationships, cuts the small group off from others, and becomes a breeding ground of neuroses. For such reasons, "the death of the family" has been widely proclaimed.

As parents ourselves, we may be somewhat defensive on this subject; after all, such criticisms touch our lives. This book is not meant as a defense of the so-called nuclear family, however, nor, certainly, is it meant to add to the criticism. Whatever the justice of the charges, they compel us to look afresh at family arrangements which most of us take for granted. Our purpose here is to focus on the role that the family has played over many centuries and in many cultures and see what lessons present themselves.

If we define the family as any regular arrangement which enables a child and one or more adults, usually close kin, to be together in the years when the child needs care, we discover that all societies have devised family systems of some sort. The particular system chosen is determined by the most profound needs of the people in a given society. The forms differ, but the needs—economic, psychological, social, political, sexual—are found among all human beings; they shape our lives. So, before we can even begin to think sensibly about the faults and attributes of what nowadays may seem to us an ordinary household, we have to ask ourselves how and why a particular form of family life should develop in a particular place and time.

From our vantage point in twentieth-century America, some of the choices that other peoples have made may seem sensible; some may seem slightly insane; some seem humane whereas others seem cruel; some exploit women, others seem to degrade men. We shall try here to avoid making such judgments, not because we lack opinions on these matters, but because we believe that it is more useful to try to understand other ways of life than it is to praise or condemn them according to our current set of standards.

In discussing the institution of the family as it has appeared and changed over the centuries, we shall be leading up to our own time and place. The origins of the kind of household that most of us are part of go back long before 1776 or 1492, deep into prehistory. We shall find in the following pages that the family has meant different things to different peoples, and we shall try to search out reasons for the variations. The differences are often striking—but so is the persistence, in the most diverse cultures, of some form of family life.

Finally, it will be left to the reader to judge how well or how poorly today's family meets his or her needs and the needs and aspirations of men and women of all ages.

November 1974
Greenburgh, New York

I

THE ROOTS
OF THE
FAMILY

O N E

The Primitive Family

The family is probably the oldest of mankind's social institutions. It existed before any state and before any church. It is found in the simplest societies, and among animals as well as among men. Howler monkeys, for example, have a special cry for "infant fallen from tree"; on hearing it, all the adult monkeys swoop down to help the little one.

Since preliterate peoples have not shown either the desire or the ability to set down the details of their private lives for the satisfaction of inquisitive outsiders, we must rely for our information about their domestic arrangements on second-hand or third-hand sources, not all as dependable as we might wish. There are historical accounts by ancient authors, tales of travelers, a few documents setting forth ancient laws, many myths and legends, quite a number of archaeological finds, and notable studies by anthropologists of peoples who live today or lived until recently much as their ancestors probably did thousands of years ago.

This material is fascinating, but not all of it is reliable—

and even when the evidence is relatively trustworthy, we usually have to add to it a dash of our own sympathetic imagination as well as an educated guess or two, to round out a picture of any group's family life. So let's keep in mind as we set out on our trek into primitive cultures that we are being guided by the judgments and opinions of people who, for all their knowledge and intelligence, cannot claim infallibility.

*

There are a few fundamental and universal facts of life that set the scene for all the varieties of family we shall be discussing. They are simple enough. Men impregnate women (though some primitive peoples, it is true, seem to have taken some time to discover or acknowledge this fact); women bear children; and human children require a long period of growth, much longer than any other animal, before they are ready to go out on their own. These are the essential bonds that tie father, mother, and child together. The study of the family is in large part the study of how people have come to terms with the basic facts of life—not only with mating, child-bearing, and child-rearing, but with work and play, as well as with survival in a sometimes hostile environment and with the critical changes that come with aging and with death.

Most scholars agree that the organization of the family in the simplest cultures stems from two biological drives—the sex drive and the hunger drive.

The sex drive, of course, brings males and females together, in twentieth-century America no less than in seventeenth-century Africa or in first-century Rome or in the animal kingdom. Unlike most animals, who have mating seasons, humans do not have a merely seasonal interest in the opposite sex. They are capable of being sexually aroused at almost any hour of any day of any month, and so it is advantageous to have a mate near at hand. Yet the sex drive by itself can be satisfied without a family structure. It is the combination of sex and hunger that has produced what we know as the family.

The hunger drive forces all animals, including humans, to develop means of keeping themselves alive. Almost invariably, this requires that individuals live fairly close to others rather than off totally by themselves. Now, if people are to live together as a group, the available labor and goods must be divided among them. Family relationships are often devised to control the division. Among the Manus, for example, marriages are looked on mainly as an economic exchange; their language has no word for "love." We modern people need to eat just as our cavemen ancestors needed to eat, and everywhere we look, we find that people have relied and still rely on kinship or descent systems of some sort to determine how the possessions they must have to get their sustenance (property, money, tools) are to be divided and passed on from one generation to the next. Today parents often go to considerable effort to leave their wealth to their children.

*

To begin at what we imagine was the beginning, what were the very earliest human families like? Here we find three conflicting theories, none of which can be absolutely confirmed or refuted, but all of which lead to the patterns of family life that we shall come upon in the next chapter, where the terms used here will be more fully explained.

1. *Matriarchy*. Aboriginal man and woman followed the example of other animals and lived in large groups or hordes. Within these groups, promiscuity was the rule, and when a child was born, no one could be certain which of the

mother's temporary partners was the child's father. He might or might not still be around. Since the basic group was the mother and her child, the child's descent was reckoned through the mother, the female line.

Now, this arrangement gave considerable power to the mother, as head of the family. Such a society might be called a *matriarchy:* power and prestige are vested in the female head of a family, the *matriarch.* Paternity is of small significance in such a society. (One tribe in the Trobriand Islands off New Guinea, possibly carrying on such a tradition, managed to eliminate the father's role completely; he was considered, not the creator of his child, but merely the "opener of the way.")

Such, at any rate, is one theory. It is not widely credited today, since investigators have not been able to find a single existing primitive tribe which practices unrestricted sexual promiscuity. Most scholars agree that there is "not a shred of genuine evidence for the notion that promiscuity ever formed a general stage in the social history of mankind." (It seems that early missionaries, on first being confronted with unfamiliar native practices, interpreted as promiscuous behavior certain set forms of courtship and marriage. Their errors should make us slow to pass judgment on "strange" customs.) Very few examples of promiscuity, incidentally, have been found in studies of apes or monkeys, those distant ancestors of ours.

2. *Patriarchy.* The earliest form of family life was the *patriarchy,* in which the father, the *patriarch,* reigned supreme. He exercised unquestioned authority over all family members—their property, their private activities, even life and death. Here, everyone would be reckoned as part of the eldest male's line of descent. The father was in charge, his wife or wives and children, and possibly his unmarried sisters and younger brothers too, lived in his house and became

part of a family line that went back to his father's father and so on.

Although aspects of such an arrangement have been found among various peoples, critics suggest that it is in fact a comparatively recent development as the human race goes; they doubt that it reaches all the way back to prehistoric times.

3. *The couple.* The earliest family resembled today's family, created by a union of one male and one female for a certain period of time. That is, two people set up a new group of their own, apart from others. Few couples may have stayed together for quite as long as the period set forth in our present marriage vow—"Till death do us part"—but, then, that particular vow is not strictly observed by all who take it today.

Defenders of this theory suggest that pairing up was a natural way to go about things, to satisfy the need for both sex and food. They believe, too, that *polygamy*—a marriage in which the man may have several wives or the woman several husbands—did not appear until a later stage in mankind's evolution, and that *monogamy*—one wife, one husband—was the basic relationship in earliest times.

These, then, are three major views of the beginnings of the family. Although they differ in important respects, they have a good deal in common. Each arrangement would aim at the same basic satisfactions, and each would achieve varying degrees of success.

One of the great and enduring benefits of family life of any kind is the sense of continuity it provides from generation to generation. In that regard, the *conjugal* family so familiar to us—husband, wife, children—which is formed at marriage and dissolved by the death or divorce or disappearance of one of the parties, suffers from obvious disadvantages. Since children tend to leave home at just about the time they become able to do a decent day's work, the family is suddenly split in two parts—in one are parents who are losing strength and energy, and in the other are children who have yet to gain experience. Moreover, a family that depends almost exclusively on the relationship of two individuals—wife and husband—can easily be broken up, by intention or by accident.

Many primitive peoples, as we shall see, relied for their sense of continuity on blood ties rather than on marriage ties. In their *consanguineous* families—groups of people connected by descent from a common parent—children and parents continued to live and function together as a team even after the children married, with the newlyweds joining either the mother's or the father's household, instead of going off to form an unconnected household of their own.

*

Let's try to maintain some humility as we think about primitive kinship arrangements. In particular, let's try to resist assuming, as some nineteenth-century writers did, that the kind of family with which we happen to be most familiar is the end product of an evolutionary process, the inevitable and generally admirable outcome of a development toward civilized behavior. Rather, let's try to think of the alternative family systems cited here as responses to specific problems faced by specific groups, deeply influenced by the conditions under which these peoples lived and the ways in which they made their living. That kind of approach can help us see our own styles of life as responses to today's problems.

However the family may have started out, it appears to have taken different forms depending on the economic needs of a particular group. We can easily see that certain conditions are more favorable to social development than others. Let's take two examples from American Indian life: whereas the Navahos were a nomadic people engaged in sheep raising over a wide area, the Pueblos lived in permanent communities. So the Pueblos had an opportunity and a need to develop complex social interrelationships that the Navahos, who came together only on ritual occasions, did not. The way people get their food has always been a powerful influence on the kind of family grouping that suits them best.

Perhaps it will clarify the point if we imagine primitive peoples moving through three economic stages. In the first stage, they get their food by hunting. In the second, they get their food by raising domestic animals and using plots of land for grazing. In the third stage, they farm the land. (More often than not, in reality, these methods of making a livelihood probably went on at the same time rather than one after the other, and it is not always easy to determine which came first.)

1. *Hunters.* For the hunter, *monogamy*—one man, one wife—made sense. While the man went forth on the difficult and dangerous work of killing wild beasts with rudimentary weapons, the woman could remain at home. Why couldn't the woman go hunting, too? Well, perhaps she did—until she found that being pregnant was an uncomfortable condition for a hunter. Once babies arrived, the mother could not readily carry one or more nursing infants along on the trek after game. Nor could she leave them behind by themselves if she wanted them to survive. So women became accustomed to tending the home territory while the men went out into the world. Women concentrated on preparing men's food, servicing their sexual and emotional needs, caring for their children.

As the children emerged from infancy in this hunting-gathering society, they could be put to use, along with their mothers, in foraging for wild vegetables, roots, herbs, and berries. Indeed, it was the women who made sure that the family would have its basic food supply even if the hunters did not bring home much game. The division of labor imposed on humans by women's singular ability to bear children enabled people to gain specialized skills. At this stage of mankind's development the family was a powerful instrument of survival.

If the hunter had tried to do everything by himself—hunt all day, make his own food, dry his own clothes, and so forth —life would have been unbearably hard. From his point of view, marriage was a convenient arrangement: a woman seems to have been valued mainly for her contributions to man's convenience, rather than cherished for herself. Among some primitive peoples, as a matter of fact, women were considered inferior and somewhat unclean. (Even in our own time, boys in New Guinea were encouraged to beat their mothers as a sign of their manliness.)

The hunter's life could not have left much room for tender impulses. One scholar writes: "Primitive marriage, as hard and dry as primitive life itself, had its origin in the most concrete and prosaic requirements." Yet some anthropologists maintain that, even in this earliest period, natural attraction and courtship played a part in marriage.

As game was exhausted in one area, the hunting family had to move on. It had little reason to spend time building fancy dwellings, and little leisure to undertake crafts such as pottery. Several families might join together for some seasons of the year, but the individual family remained the basic group. Since life was so difficult, the hunter could not feed more than one wife, whatever his inclinations; so monogamy was the rule. Women were traded between groups; a man might give away his sister in exchange for a wife.

The Shoshone Indians who lived on America's high desert plateaus in the West had to eke their livelihoods out of a harsh environment. Since it took a great deal of the barren land to feed and clothe very few people, large groups could not live together. As the young reached maturity, they went off in search of food and formed their own small, male-dominated families. Yet they also tried to keep up connections with the larger tribe, for mutual defense, for the social contacts that humans seem to require, and for religious activities. Their infrequent tribal get-togethers were occasions for new marriages—the sons and daughters of one family would connect with the daughters and sons of other families. Sometimes, as chance would have it, the sex ratio was not equal. Where there were more girls than boys, one son might marry two or more daughters—*polygyny*. Where there were more boys than girls, a daughter might marry several sons—*polyandry*. But for a hunting culture such arrangements do not seem to have been as suitable as the simple one woman–one man household.

2. *Shepherds*. Once a group began to raise domestic animals and herds, women became more valuable assets, since they could help care for the livestock and so add to the family's wealth. Now food could be stored for the future, and existence became less of a day-to-day struggle. Women found time to engage in handicrafts, making objects that could be traded for other goods. The home became a center of industry and a training school for the young, where knowledge was passed along from parent to child.

The man, with over-all responsibility for the family's herds, still remained in control, and if his family became relatively affluent he might decide, for economic reasons as well as reasons of prestige and pleasure, to take another wife, or even several others. Each of them, after all, could put in a full day's work and give him children who, in a few years, would play a part in adding to the family's wealth.

Moreover, the very possession of a large family gave a man status, much as the possession of a big house and several cars confers status in our own country today.

3. *Farmers.* The discovery of farming—for which the woman of the family, the first tiller of the soil, probably deserves credit—brought new changes to the family structure. The role of woman was much enhanced, her position in the family much improved. Because of woman's economic usefulness, it was more likely in a farming society than in a hunting or pastoral society that she would have a voice when it came to choosing a mate. (In all societies, the prestige of women has been linked to the kinds of work that they are permitted and willing to do.)

More people were needed to work the land—and the land could support more people. The value of numbers in sowing, tilling, and reaping might bring several lineage groups together into larger groups or clans, to tend their crops in common. The produce was divided among the several households, and the land itself became the clan's heritage from generation to generation.

A farm family, whether ancient or modern, is bound together by mutual dependence on its plot of land. For example, when the Shoshone Indians moved south, where they came upon irrigated land and so were able to do some farming, they began to settle in large villages which became their common territory. Since the men of the tribe (which in time became the Hopi Indians) were often away hunting while the women took care of the crops, the home was run by women—the wife, her daughters, their daughters; they formed a *matrilocal* residential group. Here, when a man married, he was taken into his wife's household, and a child's lineage was traced back through its mother.

A prime purpose unifying the farm family or clan was to

make certain that the land would be passed along intact to its descendants. In some cultures, ingenious measures were instituted to make certain this would happen. In Tibet, to cite a fairly recent example, the brothers in a family married the same woman, and all their children were regarded as the child of the eldest brother. When he died, the estate passed to "his" sons, all of whom in their turn married one wife. In this way, the family and the family's property were kept together. (In chapter 2, we shall look at other reasons for what is called *polyandry*.)

Even from so superficial a glance at different types of societies, we can see that economic conditions played a very large role indeed in determining how people went about making their family arrangements. In primitive societies, each individual's lifelong security and prospects were to a great extent in the hands of his kin.

Yet economics cannot altogether explain the peculiar powers of family life—in particular, the power of affection in human relationships, between parent and child, man and woman. Although the elements of a human being's emotional life are not as easy to pin down as the ways in which people go about providing for their physical needs, our appreciation of the family will be shallow if we do not keep them in mind.

*

One other feature common to almost all families requires mention. People in all societies, with only a very few exceptions, have gone outside their immediate groups to find a mate—a practice known as *exogamy*—rather than simply staying at home and mating with one another (*endogamy*), or even making unions of brother with sister or parent with child (*incest*). (The most famous exception to this near-universal rule was the royal family of ancient Egypt, where brothers and sisters were required to marry, ostensibly to keep blood "pure" among the ruling classes. Brother-sister marriages were also found among the Hawaiians and among the Incas of Peru.)

What is the origin of *exogamy?* Was it simply that in primitive families, where people died young, one had to go outside to find a mate? Or was it that people who grew up together in intimate physical and emotional circumstances just didn't develop a mutual sexual attraction? That seems to be the case on the Israeli *kibbutz* today, as we shall see in chapter 4. And it might explain the old Finnish custom of sending a young daughter on a long visit to distant relatives; on her return to her family, she would be received as a complete stranger, and so could be married to her brother— and keep the family and its possessions intact.

But there seems to be more than mere lack of opportunity or interest behind the general avoidance of such marriages. In particular, something more seems needed to explain the existence, among so many peoples, of powerful laws against incest and inbreeding. (Whereas exogamy refers to rules about marriage, incest has to do with sex relations among close relatives.) Why should people insist on going afield to find what they could more easily obtain right at home? And why should the prohibitions against incest be so strong? The question has fascinated students of society, and they have come up with a number of provocative theories.

One holds that primitive peoples believed that inbreeding produced monsters and idiots, and so they made laws against it. This, however, credits our ancestors with a scientific cause-and-effect approach to such matters that was probably beyond them. (Anyway, inbreeding may produce geniuses as well as idiots, and in most cases will produce neither.) More likely, primitive peoples were avoiding intrafamily marriages for other reasons, and latched on to the monster notion to justify their rules. What might these other reasons be?

If we think about children growing up in a family, be it primitive or modern, we must come to the point when the teenager's sexual urges demand an outlet. At that point, if there were no rules against a boy's mating with his blood relations, the family group might be subject to violent competition—between father and son, mother and daughter, brother and brother, sister and sister; the family's unity could be shattered. So the bans on incest might have developed out of a desire to keep the family from being torn apart from within by elemental drives.

The requirement that young men and women find mates outside their immediate households would also have brought important advantages. By intermarrying, groups could form alliances, enhancing the security of all. Poor groups, which owned little in the way of physical goods that they might trade, could exchange their women—who would thereby become hostages for more peaceable relations among neighboring peoples. Of course, any such trades would make family arrangements more complicated and call for new sets of rules. Would the husband join the wife's family, or would the wife join the husband's family, or would husband and wife go off together on their own? To which family or clan would the children belong? Different peoples found different solutions—and we shall look at a number of these solutions in the following chapter.

T W O

A Variety of Families

In chapter 1, we discussed the basic drives that have brought women and men into family groups. We also saw that these groups can take quite different forms, depending on circumstances. In this chapter, we shall look at examples of the main categories of family arrangements found in various cultures, and try to clarify the terms used to describe family types.

*

Patrilineal means the father's line, and a patrilineal society is one in which a person's descent is traced through his male forebears. In the period when the early Hebrews were a nomadic desert tribe, for example, they took great pride in a heritage transmitted through a patrilineal family tree, which they believed went back to the Biblical fathers or patriarchs Abraham, Isaac, and Jacob.

The early Hebrew society was *patriarchal*—that is, authority was vested in the chief male member of the household. It was also *patrilocal,* with wives and children gathered together in the household of the patriarch. A number of related households constituted a clan; a number of related clans made up a tribe; and in Biblical times, twelve tribes comprised the Nation of Israel. The whole nation was tied together by bonds of kinship, all its members sharing a relationship with a common ancestor. (The early Hebrew family seems to have been *polygynous*—with one husband permitted to have more than one wife, though it is unlikely that many males had the means to take advantage of the privilege.)

Sons were highly valued among the Hebrews, since it was they who would carry on the family line and rule the tribes. They were also needed to protect and tend the herds, work the fields, perform religious ceremonies, and go to battle when necessary. There was a strict division of labor between men and women. The women took care of the housework, cooked in accordance with religious law, did spinning and weaving, and sometimes sold their own products in the marketplace.

The patriarchal nature of the family was reflected in religious rituals, where men played a dominant role, and in the schooling available to boys, but not to girls. In such a society, it is not surprising that women were punished more severely than men for sexual infidelity.

The Hebrews were not the only male chauvinists of the ancient world. So powerful was the male's role among the ancient Arabs that if a husband wanted a "good seed," he could give his wife to another, respected man, in order that he might make her pregnant. A husband could also lend his wife to a guest or, if he had to make a journey, give her temporarily to a friend to use as he saw fit. The children of any such unions would belong to the husband. If, however, a wife had relations with another man without her husband's approval, that was considered adultery and punished as such.

Patriarchal societies tend to be patrilocal as well; on being married, the wife leaves her family and joins the family of her husband. Such is the practice in most African tribes—and it means an economic as well as a personal loss for the girl's family; instead of gaining a son-in-law, they are losing a daughter. The resulting feelings are sometimes symbolized by a show of hostility between the two families at the wedding ceremony. The groom's family pretends to be "capturing" the bride by force; the bride's family pretends to resist and invariably loses. After the wedding, the bride's bonds to her husband's family tend to grow stronger, while the bonds with her own family are weakened. It was much the same in ancient China, where a woman's socially acceptable role was as wife, mother, daughter-in-law—never as sister or daughter.

*

Matrilineal means the mother's line. Each person in a matrilineal system is part of a line of descent that is linked through successive generations of females. Since the mother-child bond is the most basic of all biological bonds, this is a natural arrangement. A woman's children are all members of her line or lineage, just as she and all her sisters and brothers are part of *their* mother's lineage. In a matrilineal society, your surname would be taken from your mother's family instead of your father's.

Under these circumstances, when a man marries, he does not produce children for his own lineage; only his sisters can do that. His children will belong to his wife's lineage, his mother-in-law's lineage. If you lived in such a society, you would look up to your uncle, your mother's eldest brother, as the man of the house. Whereas in a patrilineal society a man can count on his own children to carry on his line, in a matrilineal system he has to depend on his sister's children.

Some writers have speculated that matrilineal descent began among groups which did not comprehend the man's role in "making" children (after all, nine months elapse between cause and effect)—but matrilineal descent has also been found among tribes where paternity is not in doubt. Even though everybody knows who the child's father is, the child nevertheless belongs to the mother's family. In the Banks Islands, for example, the known father was prevented from eating with his son, lest the son acquire the father's character.

The Nayars, who live on the Malabar Coast of India, carried their matrilineal system to a degree that virtually eliminated the father from any but a strictly biological role in the family. A matrilineal arrangement made sense for the Nayars because the men of the village were warriors in the employ of regional rulers, and they had to be away from home for long periods either at war or on training exercises. The mostly female household kept life going in their absence. At these times, as one visitor to the tribe observed, "the mother reigns and governs"—but when the men returned, they were in charge.

On one ceremonial day, every Nayar girl between the ages of seven and twelve was married to a "ritual husband," selected on advice of the village astrologer. Each chosen male tied a gold ornament around the neck of his bride; then each couple stayed together in seclusion for three days, after which the new husband left. He might or might not thereafter become one of his wife's lovers, but in any case, he had no special rights over her and no special obligations to her. He was of no importance in himself, only as a symbol of the legitimacy of any children that his wife might bear.

In the eighteenth and nineteenth centuries, Nayar women

12766

were reported to vie with each other for "visiting husbands," taking as many as a dozen lovers apiece. The visitor arrived after supper and left before breakfast the next morning. While he was with his "wife" of the night, he left his weapons at the door of her room, to warn off other men. Although he was expected to make certain gifts to her, which added to her prestige in the village, he was under no obligation to contribute to her support; she continued to depend on her matrilineal group. And the actual father of a child, even when his identity was known for certain, had no economic, social, legal, or religious responsibilities for his offspring. That was all left to the mother's family, especially her eldest brother.

Aren't fathers in matrilineal societies ever troubled by the fact that everything they earn goes to the support of their sisters' children rather than to their own children? Evidently they are. In the Trobriand Islands off New Guinea, this feeling is sometimes satisfied by having a man's son betrothed in infancy to his sister's daughter. Now the father can be sure that whatever support he gives to his sister's family will benefit his own son. (It is not permitted among the Trobrianders for a man's daughter to marry his sister's son; that relationship is considered incestuous, much as marriages between first cousins are frowned on in twentieth-century America.)

Bronislaw Malinowski, one of this century's pioneer anthropologists, asked a Trobriander chief named Bagidou why he wanted his little son Purayasi to marry his sister's little daughter Kabwaynaya. The reply: "I wanted a daughter-in-law who would be my real kinswoman. I wanted, when I got old, to have someone of my family to look after me; to cook my food; to bring me my lime-pot and lime-stick, to pull out my gray hairs. It is bad to have a stranger do that. When it is someone of my own people, I am not afraid."

Often a matrilineal descent system is found in combination with matrilocal living arrangements (*matrilocal,* remember, means the location of the mother). Up until the fourteenth century, for example, a Japanese wife remained with her own family and her husband visited her only at night. The Japanese word for marriage meant "to slip by night into the house."

Among the Iroquois, the newly married male moved into his wife's home, which was under the control of her mother. But he continued to spend most of his time with *his* mother's group, and had responsibilities to oversee the development of his sister's sons. As one observer of such a society put it, "A man seeks companionship with other men, loves his sister, and sleeps with his wife."

A visitor to the matrilocal Ashanti tribe in Africa described a typical evening scene: "One will see children running between the houses carrying dishes and bowls of food. They are taking it from the mother's house to the father's house."

An anthropologist who lived with a people known as the Rotuma, on a tiny island north of Fiji, gave this account of their matrilocal practices: "The husband only remains in his wife's *hoag* [hut] during her life. On her death, he is pushed out of one doorway of the house as the corpse is carried out through the other, signifying that he has no right in it." His children, however, remain behind with their mother's people.

In the Caroline Islands, too, children were considered real relatives only to the mother; to the father, they were strangers. Thus, in any war between two kinship groups, a father and his son might have found themselves on opposing sides.

A favorite example of the matrilineal family in practice is the Hopi tribe, found in the deserts of northern Arizona. The

Hopi household is likely to contain a mature woman, her daughters, and possibly her granddaughters. They live together in the same home for their entire lives, and all their female children remain there with them. As for the husbands, they are mere guests in their wives' households. They may help to support their wives, but their closest connections are with the homes of their own mothers, where they were brought up. It follows that the influence of women tends to be stronger in matrilineal than in patrilineal societies.

The closest of all relationships among the Hopi is that between a mother and her daughter. They are tied for life. At a very early age, a girl is put to doing household chores—taking care of younger children, carrying water, grinding and cooking corn, and so forth—all under her mother's supervision. She may have a bond of affection with her father, but it is rarely as strong as the bond with her mother. As for boys, their upbringing is supervised not by their own fathers but by their mother's brother. He is the disciplinarian for his sister's children—but not for his own children.

Now, we would not expect a matrilineal marriage to be very intense or enduring. After all, the husband's main affections and loyalties remain in his mother's home, not his wife's: "Your sister is always your sister; tomorrow your wife may be another man's wife." A blood relationship counts for more than a marriage relationship. In his wife's house, a man is always something of an outsider. In arguments, women tend to take their brothers' part against their husbands', blood ties proving stronger than marriage ties.

So, although nearly all the Hopi marry, their divorce rate is high. Owing to the husband's lack of authority and his role as outsider, marriage ties are loose. It's easy to get a divorce. If the husband is dissatisfied, he simply goes back to his mother, his "real" home. If the wife is dissatisfied, all she has to do to end her marriage is place her husband's belongings outside the door of her house. A divorce in such a society creates no great emotional traumas; both parties find themselves back at home, among their loved ones.

(Among some primitive tribes, efforts were made to control divorce, in the interests of justice. In one, a wife who was deserted without just cause was entitled to take "all the personal property of her husband, except one drinking cup and the cloth round his loins." This rule may remind some divorced American males of their personal experience.)

Despite what may seem to us weak bonds between husband and wife, father and children, this form of family based on blood ties has proved to have considerable strengths. The clan, which claims descent from a common ancestor, has the inescapable responsibility to stay together, to protect the children and care for the aged. It is not a matter of choice; a person is part of his or her clan from birth until death. Even when a marriage is broken by divorce, the home is not broken; it remains intact. If a parent goes away or dies, the children may grieve, but they have the security of knowing that their home will remain much as it has always been.

Given our own values, we are likely to feel that there is some warmth lacking in the attachments of Hopi men and women—but it would be rash for us to discount the benefits that they find in their matrilineal system.

*

Polygyny, a word borrowed from the Greek, is the practice of a man having more than one wife. Once widespread, polygyny can still be found in parts of Africa and the Middle East. One present-day chieftain in the United Republic of Cameroon, for example, has six wives and twenty-five children. Some researchers attribute this arrangement in part to the differing sexual needs and desires of males and females; but as we shall see, there are other reasonable explanations for it. Whatever the reasons, polygyny has generally been accompanied by a low view of womankind and the subservience of wives to their husbands and masters. Among the Fiji Islanders, for example, all wives but the first were treated as slaves.

A good example of polygyny is the Baganda tribe as it existed at the end of the nineteenth century in Central Africa, around what is now Uganda. Among the Bagandas, the king had hundreds of wives, tribal chieftains had dozens, and commoners had two or three. As this suggests, the number of wives was a sign of a man's prestige and wealth.

Generally, for polygyny to be feasible, there must be a greater number of females than males—and indeed, in Baganda at the turn of the century there were three times as many women as men. This was the outcome of centuries of excessive male deaths—at birth, in warfare, in risky occupations, in religious sacrifices, in political executions. (Whether the Baganda practiced polygyny because they had fewer men than women, or whether males were killed in order to sustain polygyny, remains a complicated question.)

Women were considered a form of property, and the purchase of a bride was an economic investment as well as a means of cementing alliances between groups of kin. Once the bride was chosen and the bride price negotiated and paid by the man's relatives to the woman's relatives (the higher the price, the greater the bride's prestige), the bride was anointed with butter and fed with goodies to make her more desirable. On the day before the marriage, she was washed thoroughly by her husband-to-be's sisters (who took the opportunity to inspect her for infirmities). A man's first wife would normally become his main wife; those who followed were likely to have less of a voice in the running of the household.

The bride's chief value in the Baganda family was as a bearer of children and a worker. If she did not become pregnant within a few weeks after marriage—with the help of drugs, charms, medicine men, and the village gods—the husband was bound to be disappointed in his investment. A woman who proved unable to bear children at all could not expect to remain a favored wife for long. Sterility in a wife was not tolerated.

In addition to producing children, the wife's main role in Baganda society was as a gardener. The new wife was given a hoe by the bridegroom's mother, a symbol of her duties and her major lifetime tool. She began work in the family garden each day at sunrise and continued past sunset— whereas her husband might put in a few hours of labor in the morning and the afternoon as the spirit moved him. Since a good plantain garden, tended by one woman, could support several people, tribesmen had a strong economic incentive to get as many healthy, hard-working wives as they could afford. An enterprising male might bring into his household, in addition to a primary wife and subsidiary wives, his un-married female relatives, all of whom would be expected to pitch in and help make him prosperous.

When a husband died, his first wife usually joined the family of the brother who lived closest to her late husband's grave, which she was obliged to tend. The other wives, too, were claimed by male relatives, who prized them for their productivity.

In obtaining a wife, a man purchased not only the right to her labor but in most cases the right to consider her children part of his family strain. Since it was considered shameful to die without children of one's own, in some tribes it was a man's duty to marry his brother's widow and beget children in behalf of the dead brother. This indicates that kinship was considered a more important relationship than marriage. As one tribe member remarked, "I can get a new wife any time, but I have only one father."

The husband also had sexual rights to his wife. Any woman caught in adultery might be severely beaten—and her husband might kill the offending man. (He would probably hold back on killing the wife, since that would mean an economic loss for himself.) But the polygynous man generally had sexual duties of his own to perform. In some tribes of Sierra Leone, a man had to spend three days, in turn, with each of his wives. If he did not favor any one of them sexually even once during her turn, that might be grounds for her leaving him. In other, possibly more sophisticated tribes, the husband was supposed to give each wife what she *needed,* rather than perform according to any prescribed order, an approach that sounds very up-to-date.

No one will be surprised to learn that a polygynous household with its several competing women, even though they might be segregated in separate rooms or separate huts, could be a hotbed of conflict. Although the first wife customarily had the greatest authority, she might readily become upset by the suspicion that her husband was paying undue attention to a new, younger, more alluring wife, or showing preference for another wife's children over her own. There might be jockeying among wives for special favors from the husband, leading to strained relationships and periods of tension around the house.

Still, observers have discerned numerous advantages in a tribe's polygynous arrangement, for both women and men. By giving the man a larger family, as we have noted, such an arrangement gave him greater prestige and greater wealth, along with variety in his sex life. Since he had several wives at his disposal, he didn't have to remain celibate during any one wife's lengthy nursing period—as long as three or four years, during which she was customarily expected to refrain from sex.

From the woman's point of view, polygyny eased her workload—which probably explains why some women encouraged their husbands to take additional wives. Polygyny gave women a chance to combine a career in the garden with household and child-rearing tasks, since they could rotate their jobs. Despite the element of competition, it provided each wife with companionship. And it gave each the assurance that her children would be taken care of when she was ill or having another child. So, for wives as well as husbands, polygyny appears to have had (and, in some cultures, may still have) its attractive side.

*

Polyandry is a Greek word that means having many husbands. It is a rare situation and tends to be associated with three conditions:

First, there is usually a shortage of women in the society, making it impossible for every male to find a wife of his own. If several men weren't permitted to marry the same woman, they might find themselves involved in bloody competition for the few women available. In some places, a shortage of women seems to have been brought on by the practice of female infanticide—the killing of some girls in infancy—but there is no absolutely clear relationship between infanticide and polyandry. Infanticide has been found in China without polyandry, whereas polyandry has been found in Tibet without infanticide. All we are safe in concluding is that a society which has a surplus of women would probably not find it useful to practice polyandry.

Second, the polyandrous society is likely to be poor, so poor that one man alone cannot support a wife and children. Under these circumstances, rapid population growth would only make matters worse by creating more mouths to feed. The allocation of one wife to several husbands is a way of keeping down the population as well as providing a team of breadwinners for each family unit. (However, that is not to suggest that all polyandrous societies are in fact poor.)

Third, and connected to the last point, each family may wish to pass along its precious land intact from generation to generation. If all the male offspring of a family (all the brothers) marry the same woman and live as a single economic unit, there will be no reason to subdivide the family plot.

Let's have a look at an example. As polyandry is practiced in Tibet, each household has one wife. She has been married to the eldest brother, and his brothers are her inferior husbands. Under the harsh conditions of Tibet, this arrangement affords protection to the family's woman and children; when one man has to go on a journey, the household is likely to have other men in residence.

Every child, no matter who his or her real father is, belongs to the eldest male, the head of the family. When the eldest dies, his property, his authority, and his widow are all passed along to the next eldest. This is similar to the practice among some peoples of a younger brother marrying the widow of an older brother; it is known as the *levirate*. Even in places where polyandry is not the rule, a younger brother may discard his own wife in order to marry an older brother's widow, in the interests of perpetuating his brother's family line.

The Toda family in southern India is a classic example of polyandrous society. The Todas are a pastoral tribe who have been isolated from the rest of Indian society for hundreds of years. Up until this century, they practiced female infanticide, with some girl babies being smothered at birth. Despite this unwholesome custom, they are a peaceful and dignified people, herdsmen who depend for their livelihood on the raising of buffalo and on dairying. The buffalo is a sacred creature to them, and its care—undertaken exclusively by males—is considered to be a priestly function.

Marriages among the Todas are arranged very early, sometimes at the age of two or three. The Toda girl who marries one brother in a family thereby becomes the wife of all the brothers, including those not yet born. In this system of *fraternal* polyandry, all the brothers share equally in all marital privileges, without apparent jealousy. When one of the brothers is with the wife, he places his cloak and staff outside his hut as a signal to the others not to barge in. Where husbands live at some distance from each other, the wife usually moves in with each for a month at a time. A man in search of a wife or mistress may either buy a woman from her husband or take his place in an existing family as one more husband.

When a wife becomes pregnant, no one is interested in determining who the biological father is—that could be a difficult job of detection where there are four or five brothers to choose from. Instead, one of the brothers, usually the eldest, is chosen to act as the recognized father. After two or three children have been born, this honor and responsibility may be passed along to another brother as other offspring arrive.

Children in the Toda family are well treated. After all, they each have several fathers or father-uncles to play with them. Girls learn early to clean, mend, pound grain, carry water, and embroider. By the time a girl reaches adolescence, she is likely to be married and to have had numerous sexual encounters. That is true for the adolescent boy as well, since he is entitled to all marital favors from the wife of his elder brothers from the hour that he becomes able to enjoy them and is inclined to do so.

Women are subordinate to men in the Toda culture—as indicated by the fact that the women of the tribe must kiss the men's feet on ceremonial occasions. When a girl marries, she moves to the village of her husband—a patrilocal arrangement. Whereas the man thinks of himself as having a priestly function as he attends to the tribe's buffalo, the woman's tasks are all menial.

Whatever else the woman may lack, she is guaranteed sexual relations in abundance with a variety of partners throughout her life. (A less favorable view of the Toda wife's situation is to see her as a sexual object, open to exploitation by every male in the tribe.) There is no concept of adultery in Toda society; men and women share a freedom in sex matters which, as one observer has noted, is "unthinkable to the Western mind." If a woman's husband should die, the pangs of widowhood are soothed by the certain knowledge that one of his brothers will promptly fill his role in principle, as he has been doing all along in practice.

Since World War II, there have been significant changes in the way of life of the Todas which are affecting their polyandrous relationships. For example, with the ending of female infanticide, more wives have become available and each man has a better chance of finding a woman of his own —who, by tradition, he naturally will share with his brothers, even though they too have their own wives. This has resulted in an unusual combination of polyandry and polygyny, or group marriage—a form of marriage, incidentally, which has its champions today in our own country.

*

It is worth keeping in mind, as we contemplate the diversities of family life, that every arrangement we have discussed represents an effort by a society to meet its people's needs. Every family type, whether patrilineal or matrilineal, whether polyandrous or polygynous or monogamous, must, if it is to endure, provide a setting for men and women to mate and raise their young. It must be responsive to their economic needs. It must embody rules of courtship, legitimacy, inheritance, and the obligations of kin that are in accord with the society's traditions. The family, whatever its form, is society's device for assuring its own well-being.

II

KIN,

CHURCH,

AND STATE

THREE

The Family in Western Civilization

In every part of the world, from primitive times onward, human beings have attempted to satisfy their deepest needs through their families; and the families have taken different forms depending on the conditions with which different peoples have had to come to terms. That is the message we hope came through in the first two chapters. The kind of family that is most familiar to us, the one that most of us have lived in all our lives, is part of the history of Western civilization, and in this chapter we shall pick out from that long history a few of the major influences that went into making the kind of family we know today.

*

The upper-class Roman family, in the years when Rome was setting out on its march to greatness, was patriarchal and patrilineal. It usually contained three generations and was an economic, educational, legal, and religious institution all rolled into one. Family gods were worshipped at home; most children were taught at home; everyone in the household worked for the benefit of all; the father handed down punishment and rewards.

In early Rome, everybody belonged to a household of some sort, under control of the *paterfamilias,* or the father of the family. Among wealthy Romans, even slaves were considered part of the household. When a girl married, she became a member of her husband's family, though the new couple would most likely settle down in living quarters of their own.

Marriages came early in Rome—usually in the teens. They were arranged by the heads of the families concerned, sometimes with the assistance of professional matchmakers. The main parties to a marriage ceremony were not the two people getting married but their kin, who were thereby entering into an alliance of sorts. Among the upper classes (and most of what we know of Roman life relates to the upper classes, not to the majority of the people), the primary purpose of marriage was to assure sound economic, social, and political connections for the participating families. By arranging their children's marriages early, parents forestalled the risk that the boys and girls might find unsuitable partners.

The future wife and husband, whose fates were sometimes decided before they were old enough to understand fully what was happening, had little or no say in the matter. As the Roman philosopher Seneca would comment in Rome's later years: "Any animal or slave, every article of clothes or dish is tested before purchase, but never the bride by her groom. Any vices she may have of passion, stupidity, misshapedness or evil breath one learns after marriage." The bride, to be sure, was just as ignorant about her groom's breath as he was about hers—but most Romans evidently did not feel that mattered much.

In theory, and often in practice, the Roman father had absolute control over his children and his son's children—*patria potestas,* the Romans called it, or roughly translated, Poppa Power. A newborn baby was placed at its father's feet. If the father took it up, it became part of his family. If not, it might be exposed on the roadside, either to perish or to be taken away by someone, perhaps as a slave.

Even after a boy was married, he was not permitted to hold property of his own; his father controlled his finances. A father could arrange for his children's divorce, with or without their consent. He could even sell a son if he felt he had cause—though this was rarely done. Finally, the *paterfamilias* had the ultimate power, after consultation with a family council, to condemn to death any of his children—though this power, too, must have been exercised only in exceedingly rare circumstances. Although permitted by law, it was frowned on by custom.

There was no limit to the punishment a Roman master could impose on his slaves. Moreover, if a master was murdered, all his slaves were put to death without the bother of a trial—an effective way to discourage slaves from plotting against masters. In A.D. 61, a wealthy official named Pedanius Secundus was killed by one of his slaves; his entire household of four hundred slaves was executed in retaliation.

A Roman husband could divorce his wife for adultery, as well as for preparing poison, drinking wine, and making duplicate house keys. Although he also had the right to divorce her at his whim, without cause, such an action would likely have been disapproved of by his kinsmen.

There were strict rules of sexual behavior—at least for women. A wife caught having relations with a man other than her husband was liable to immediate death—but that rule did not apply to adulterous husbands. The philosopher Cato remarked to a friend: "If you were to catch your wife in adultery, you would kill her with impunity without trial; but if she were to catch you, she would not dare to lay a finger upon you."

Family life in ancient Rome was thoroughly shaken up by Rome's three wars with Carthage, the Punic Wars, which took men away from Rome for many years during the third and second centuries B.C. The women left at home had to take on fresh responsibilities—and along with these responsibilities came a certain amount of freedom. The men, meanwhile, were availing themselves of greater sexual freedom abroad.

As Rome's wars and conquests continued and great wealth poured into the country from around the globe, the style of life changed, and the once-powerful domestic ties were weakened. The symptoms of family breakdown were many: more divorces; fewer children; introduction among the upper classes of a form of "companionate marriage," in which the bonds between husband and wife were quite loose and could be easily dissolved, and no children were desired; an erosion of the rules against adultery, abortion, and prostitution (the satirist Juvenal wrote: "Chastity has long since left the earth. No woman is content with a single lover nowadays"); increased juvenile delinquency as the young broke away from their parents; and a general deterioration of respect for the once-powerful family.

In the first century A.D., in an effort to repair the domestic disarray and quell the moral laxity of the Romans the Emperor Augustus put forward new laws designed to restore the strength of marriage and family ties. In accord with Roman tradition, these laws weighed more heavily on women than on men. A childless woman between the ages of twenty and fifty was given two years to remarry if her husband died; in the case of divorce, she had only eighteen months. (Augustus himself, for all his concern for the family, never married.) But not even the power of the state could restore the Roman family to the preeminent position it had held in the days of the Republic. Too many other influences were at work.

*

The rise of Christianity, which occurred during the centuries of the Roman Empire's dissolution, had a far-reaching impact on attitudes toward family life in the West.

For the early Christian fathers, marriage was not a desirable condition. Some saw it as flatly immoral, believing that all pleasures of the flesh were corrupt, that sexual attraction was evil. They strongly condemned adultery, masturbation, sexual perversions, contraception, and abortion—and did not stop there. The reading of "lascivious" books, the singing of "wanton" songs, the dancing of "suggestive" dances, the wearing of "improper" clothing, bathing in mixed company, going to the theater—all were condemned. For these first Christians, abstinence from all forms of sex and the avoidance of any kind of sexual temptation were much to be desired.

Now, a person who is antagonistic to sex in all its forms is not likely to be a champion of married life. One scholar has observed that the early Christians "seemed to long for that nomadic state in which man would ultimately neither desire nor possess a hearth nor a home, and would no longer concentrate his affection or search for his happiness in the family state."

St. Paul, the most influential of the early Christian converts, and a bachelor, wrote: "I would that all men were even as I myself . . . I say therefore to the unmarried and widows, it is good for them to abide even as I." However, living during a period of sexual immorality, Paul recognized the powers of sex, and preferred that they be contained within the family rather than loosed altogether—for, after all, promiscuity meant sin and damnation. So he added the famous advice: "But if they cannot contain, let them marry; for it is better to marry than to burn."

The Christian fathers eventually settled for two levels of sexual morality—one for clergy and nuns, who were obligated to be celibate; and one for ordinary folk, who were encouraged to marry and have children, but who were warned against seeking satisfactions for their sexual appetites outside of marital intercourse or even within marriage if the purpose was not to conceive children.

The attitudes of the early Christian thinkers toward women were complicated and somewhat confusing, even to themselves. These pious men seemed to be torn between two views of woman: as a descendant of Eve the temptress, and as a symbol of purity, on the order of the Virgin Mary. St. John Chrysostom, who lived in the fourth century and was the most influential of the Greek Church fathers, looked upon woman as a "necessary evil, a natural temptation, a desirable calamity, a domestic peril, a deadly fascination, and a painted ill."

Paul left no doubt that in his opinion the good Christian household was one in which the male was dominant. He called on wives "to be sober, to love their husbands, to love their children, to be discreet, chaste, keepers at home, good, obedient to their husbands."

As the church gained in power, it began to exercise various kinds of control over marriages—having a priest officiate at the ceremony, adopting a formal liturgy, setting down rules as to whom Christians might marry and whom they might not marry (heretics and infidels and blood relations were out), establishing stringent requirements for separation.

It was in part an outgrowth of Christianity's divided attitude toward sex, women, and the family that, in the chivalric codes of the Middle Ages, romantic love was cut off altogether from marriage. Since one was not expected to find romance at home, knights made strenuous efforts to become enamored of other people's wives rather than their own, and operated under the belief or delusion that their lady loves were a hundred percent pure and their own sentiments were a hundred percent high-minded. The notion that sexual affection might be an accepted part of marriage did not gain currency until the sixteenth and seventeenth centuries.

Gradually, over a period of many centuries, the controls that groups of kinsmen had exercised over family life, among the Romans and also among the barbarian tribes that invaded the Roman Empire in its decline, were taken into the hands of church officials, often backed up by state officials.

In eleventh-century Britain, for example, King Canute handed down a set of stringent laws, in accord with church teachings, to regulate his subjects' sex lives. A woman found to be having relations with a man other than her husband was to lose not only all her worldly possessions but her nose and ears as well. In an alliance of church and state, the penalty was to be enforced by the bishop.

In England, around the twelfth century there began the "golden period of canon rule," when the church enforced upon the entire population the duty to marry and breed. So the family patriarch was forced to give up some of his powers, and the family was increasingly compelled to operate under rules imposed from outside. The independence of kinship groups, bound by blood ties, was inevitably undermined. The influence of religious institutions on marriage, divorce, and family relations in general, though by no means what it used to be, remains part of our contemporary heritage.

*

Among the innumerable transformations that overtook Europe after the so-called Dark Ages, several are of particular significance for students of the family.

Between the thirteenth and seventeenth centuries, feudal society prevailed throughout most of Europe. The king was at the top of the social-economic-political pyramid; the lords or major landowners of the country paid him allegiance and, in turn, were paid allegiance by the people who lived and worked on their lands. Whereas the rich might live in mansions, a poor family was lucky to have a single room. A prosperous feudal household might include the husband, his wife, their children, the husband's widowed mother or old father, and a number of servants. Portraits of family groups at home attained extraordinary popularity in the sixteenth and seventeenth centuries—evidence that the concept of the family was gaining in importance. Here is the caption that went with one such picture of a well-to-do merchant, his wife, and their two young children: "Happy is he who obeys the labor of Heaven and devotes the best years of his life in serving God, his family, and his king."

One of the main underpinnings of the feudal system was *primogeniture,* a form of inheritance by which all the family's land was passed along to the eldest son after his father's death. Obviously, this was an effort to keep the family's holdings intact, rather than have them parceled out among several children. (For as far back as history takes us, land and family have been intertwined. In ancient Egypt, where daughters usually inherited a share of the estate, the family property was kept whole by marriages between sisters and brothers.) Illegitimate offspring, such as the fruits of an affair between the scion of a well-to-do family and a peasant girl, were entitled to nothing in feudal times. Indeed, one of the prime functions of the family since its beginnings has been to certify a child's legitimacy, its claim to the family name, status, and possessions.

(The effects of primogeniture were felt in many ways. It has been suggested, for example, that the contrast between the rapid industrialization of Japan in the nineteenth century and the laggard pace of China was related to their inheritance traditions. In China, the family inheritance was shared by all the sons in the family, which naturally dispersed the family's capital. In Japan, on the other hand, the oldest son was usually the sole beneficiary; in this way, wealth was accumulated and could be readily invested in machinery and factories.)

While primogeniture did succeed in keeping the land whole, it discouraged the younger children from marrying early, since they had no means of their own; and it encouraged them to seek wives from well-to-do families who would come to them with substantial dowries. Pounds and shillings were the major considerations in many marriages. Whereas the family heir was likely to have a large family, his younger brothers were likely to have smaller ones. One seventeenth-century writer protested: "There is not only great vanity in giving the better part of one's estate to the eldest son of the family, to maintain him in splendor and eternalize his name; there is even injustice. What have the younger sons done to be treated like this?"

In time, however, primogeniture proved to be an incentive to the brightest, most energetic younger sons to go off and make careers for themselves away from the family lands, to start their own families and become part of a mobile labor force that contributed to the growth of towns. One writer notes that, from the late Middle Ages, primogeniture "provided a stimulus to younger sons. Knowing that the estate would go to their eldest brother, they often prepared themselves for some profession, the civil service or the army. The heir, on the other hand, lacking any incentive 'to get out and hustle,' was often said to be 'untaught and good for nothing.' "

In many English families, children were sent away at an early age, to serve as apprentices and learn a trade. An Italian traveler of the fifteenth century cited this practice as evidence of a lack of family feeling. He wrote: "The want of affection in the English is strongly manifested towards their children; for after having kept them at home till they arrive at the age of seven or nine years at the utmost, they put them out, both males and females, to hard service in the houses of other people, binding them generally for another seven or nine years. And these are called apprentices, and during that time they perform all the most menial offices."

As towns sprung up in Europe, some of the functions which had traditionally been performed by the kinship group began to be taken over by newly created town institutions. As official police forces developed, for example, the individual no longer had to rely on his own kin for protection. Gradually, too, schools began to replace the apprenticeship system.

Throughout the Middle Ages it was generally understood that the aged, the needy, the handicapped would be cared for by their own families. But in the town many people were far from home, and so institutions, such as almshouses or poorhouses, were created to care for those in need. In some countries, such as England, this "secularization" process was part of a movement to wrest control of family life away from the church and transfer it to the developing state.

The enactment in England in 1597 of the "poor laws," which made it the explicit responsibility of the head of a family to support his dependent children and parents, can be taken as a sign that bonds of kinship were getting weaker. After all, if family groups were in fact supporting their needy, as they traditionally had, what reason would there have been to write such a responsibility into the law? Why would the state have to step in?

*

Whatever the other changes in the family over these centuries, they do not seem to have done much for the status of women. Long after the Middle Ages, marriages continued to be arranged, sometimes at a very young age and with no regard for personal preference. (There is evidence that at least one sixteenth-century girl knew her own mind and, "fancying a nice boy of ten-eleven," enticed him into marrying her, with a gift of two apples.)

The Marquis of Halifax explained to his daughter in 1687: "It is one of the disadvantages belonging to your sex, that young women are seldom permitted to make their own choice; their friends' care and experience are thought safer guides to them than their own fancies, and their modesty often forbiddeth them to refuse when their parents recommend, though their inward consent may not entirely go along with it."

Although the patriarchal household was not as strong as in Roman times, wives were still clearly subordinated to their mates, and females were not taken altogether seriously. In a letter to his son written in 1748, Lord Chesterfield advised: "A man of sense only trifles with them [girls], as he does with a sprightly forward child; but he neither consults them about nor trusts them with serious matters, though he often makes them believe that he does both, which is the thing in the world that they are proud of . . ."

In this view, girls were to be lightly courted and, once

won, treated as being irresponsible when it came to "serious" matters. Under the English Common Law as formulated in the eighteenth century, a woman upon being married "dissolved her legal personality into that of her husband." A wife could not keep any earnings, enter into any contracts, or testify in any court on her own. For the husband's part, he was responsible for the support and welfare of his wife and children, and for making sure they didn't get into any trouble.

Where sex was concerned, there was a conspicuous double standard: what was permitted to young men was unforgivable in young women. One English lord counseled young wives to overlook their husbands' episodes of straying from the marriage bed: "Remember, that next to the danger of committing the fault yourself, the greatest is that of seeing it in your husband. Do not seem to look or hear that way."

A few women protested. In 1700, an English schoolteacher wrote: "And if a woman can neither Love nor Honour, she does ill in promising to Obey."

The remarkable English feminist Mary Wollstonecraft wrote in her *Vindication of the Rights of Women:* "Would men but generously snap our chains, and be content with rational fellowship instead of slavish obedience, they would find us more observant daughters, more affectionate sisters, more faithful wives, more reasonable mothers—in a word, better citizens."

Such pleas went largely unheeded—but women, too, were finding new areas of independence, owing to changes in living styles that were sweeping over entire societies.

The movement away from the land into fast-growing cities was accelerated during the eighteenth and nineteenth centuries. Englishmen flocked to London and Birmingham. Many Europeans went much further afield, leaving the countries of their birth for such booming metropolises as New York and Chicago. In their new homes, they were compelled to develop new family arrangements.

New machines transformed entire economies. New industries sprung up; new factories were built; an entire new working class was created during these centuries. The old-style family of perhaps a dozen people proved unsuited to the changed conditions. On the feudal estate, large families had been an advantage because everybody could work and there was no shortage of living space. But the factory could not guarantee wages to every member of a family. Usually, the husband and father had to support all the others, and an ordinary worker's pay was not enough for the upkeep of more than his wife and children, if that. Whereas on the farm every member of the family had been a producer, in the city all but one were consumers, at least until children were old enough, at age ten or thereabouts, to be sent into the mines or mills.

Moreover, city living simply did not provide the room that country living did. Homes tended to be cramped and dark, no inducement to inviting uncles, aunts, and cousins to come live there too. Also, there was much more movement from place to place in search of work, and this mobility, too, disrupted relations among kin. Relatives who were once accustomed to living near one another were dispersed around the country.

So the large old-style families were broken up as young people went off, away from the control of their father, and as contacts with brothers, cousins, grandparents became less frequent and less close. While the church took over some of the family's functions as rulemaker in the area of morals, the state took over more and more of its social functions, such as providing for the needy and the sick. Often the state's activities were welcomed, even demanded by the citizenry—but sometimes they were resisted. As we shall see in the following chapter, relations between the state and the family, never entirely amicable, can become a source of exasperation for everyone concerned.

FOUR

The Family and the State

Given the intimate and intricate ties between the family and the society in which it exists, we need not be surprised to learn that every state attempts to regulate family life to some degree. Virtually all governments have laid down rules which touch the most private aspects of people's lives, making some kinds of sexual behavior lawful and others unlawful, some children legitimate and others illegitimate, seeking to control human drives in behalf of a stable society.

Among primitive peoples, who have no "government" in our sense of the word, the family plays the roles that we are accustomed to assign to official bodies. Punishment for even so grave a crime as murder may be left to the individual family or kinship group. The story is told of an Eskimo mother who strangled her son in his sleep because he had become a great nuisance to the community. Eskimos are far from a bloodthirsty people; indeed, they are singled out for their indulgence toward their children—but, in this case, the mother may have felt that death at her hands was preferable to exile by the entire community and even crueler death in the Arctic wastes.

In our own country and time, the state acts through the family to make people "behave." Nowhere in the United States, for example, can a man legally have more than one wife, or a woman more than one husband. Everywhere, getting married requires a license and getting divorced requires legal proceedings. Everywhere, parents are held responsible for the care of their children. Adultery is a criminal offense, at least on some statute books. Single people are taxed more heavily than married people—an inducement to marriage for the thrifty. And so it goes.

We hear few protests over such intrusions by lawmakers into our private lives. We take them for granted. In part, that is because most of us acknowledge that the society does have a legitimate interest in encouraging certain types of behavior and discouraging other types, as long as the rules are not onerous and can be adapted to changing circumstances. By and large, the existing rules reflect a broad consensus of what family life ought to be like. Most Americans, for example, would undoubtedly agree that a stable marriage and the rearing of children by their parents are highly desirable objectives. When public attitudes change, as they conspicuously have in recent years with regard to such matters as divorce, the laws tend to change too. For the most part, then, our lawmakers are not imposing their own notions on the majority but are only confirming generally held views about marriage, child support, and so forth.

Whereas changes in family relations tend to come gradually, history is filled with proposals that would alter radically the way people live together, with a view to creating a new, "superior" kind of society. In Plato's ideal society, to take a favorite example, no father was to know his own child.

Conception would take place at certain set festivals each year. Children born at the wrong time of the year would be eliminated. Children born at the right time would be taken from their mothers at birth and raised by specially designated persons.

Theorists of the French Revolution, for their part, sought to make marriage and family obligations a private matter; they wanted to break down existing conventions, even though these were accepted by the great majority of Frenchmen. On the other hand, Fascist regimes of the 1930's preached strict family rules and child-bearing as duties to the regime. "German girls!" exhorted Adolf Hitler. "Remember that you are destined to become a German mother. In my state the mother will be the most important woman citizen." In China today, the welfare of the state takes precedence over the desires of individuals in such matters as divorce.

Behind all such cases is the conviction that what concerns the family concerns the state, that the way people conduct their personal affairs is vital to the proper functioning of the entire society.

In this chapter, we shall look at two of this century's efforts to influence family life—in the Soviet Union and in the Israeli *kibbutz,* or collective agricultural settlement. The settings differ in a multitude of ways, but they do have in common the attempt to impose dramatic changes on domestic customs. Their experience has a good deal to tell us about the flexibility of the family and its persistence.

*

Many of the early leaders of the 1917 Communist Revolution in Russia did not look kindly upon the family. It was the revolutionists' avowed intention, after all, to create a new society, new men and women whose primary loyalties would be to the state. They feared that the family would be an obstacle on the road to that goal.

Communist theorists argued that the family was a selfish institution. It confined people's affections to a handful of relatives rather than dispersing them outward, to the entire nation; it encouraged parents to hoard material goods for their own comfort and for the future comfort of their children rather than cooperate in behalf of the society; in every way, it turned citizens' attentions and actions inward rather than outward. The Communists condemned the family as a bulwark of religion and "reactionary" impulses.

The famous Bolshevik leader Nikolai Bukharin called the family "a formidable stronghold of all the turpitudes of the old regime." Alexandra Kollontay, a leading Communist expert in the field, wrote in 1919: "The family has ceased to be a necessity both for its members and for the state." And all through the 1920's, party leaders continued to inveigh against it. A writer in Leningrad predicted that, as socialism developed, the family would "die out."

"The home life of a woman is a daily sacrifice to a thousand unimportant trivialities," wrote Lenin, the preeminent Bolshevik leader. It was his hope that women, no longer chained to household chores, would be free to work in factories—a crucial need in the early years of the Soviet regime. As Lenin declared: "Every cook must learn to run the state."

In accord with such views, the new Communist government in the U.S.S.R. enacted a number of measures designed to weaken the authority of the family and change relations between husband and wife and parents and children. As one observer put it, "The old dictum that a woman's place was in the home was replaced by the notion that a woman's place was everywhere except in the home."

The new Family Code was indeed revolutionary. All legal requirements for marriage were abolished. Relationships between men and women would be left to the individuals concerned; they would come together and part as they pleased —without interference from any official body. A wife would no longer have to adopt her husband's name. If a couple wished to have children, they could; if not, contraceptives and abortion would be readily available. Adoption was prohibited, in order to discourage childless couples from starting new families of their own. Both parties to any arrangement would be self-supporting; and both were obliged to contribute to the support of their children. Large inheritances were done away with; property above 10,000 rubles would go to the state on the owner's death.

Since it was generally agreed that fathers and mothers did more harm than good, children were to be taken out of the household at an early age, and imbued with Communist values. Their upbringing would be left largely to public institutions, such as nurseries, schools, and recreational facilities. Some party spokesmen declared flatly that every child was in fact the property of the state and ought to be removed from the parents' house altogether and placed in a special "children's town" where she or he could be raised to be the kind of citizen needed and desired by state officialdom.

Others held a more temperate view. An early Commissar of Education wrote: "It would be idiotic to separate children from their parents by force. But when, in our communal houses, we have well-organized quarters for children . . . there is no doubt that the terms 'my parents,' 'our children,' will gradually fall out of usage."

How, in fact, did the attack on the Russian family work out? Not at all as the early Soviet planners believed it would.

The large, autocratic families of Czarist times were

broken up, but otherwise the planners' hopes were disappointed. Within a few years, inheritance was again permitted; there was simply too much resistance to turning over one's property to the state and leaving one's children to make their way without as good a start as possible. The rule against adoption was gradually relaxed, as it became evident that there were not enough public facilities to care properly for homeless infants in the period after the disruptions of World War I. Soon, instead of parentless babies being passed along to the state for care, the state was farming them out to private families. In 1926, adoption was again acknowledged as a legal act.

The free and easy attitude toward divorce also worked out undesirably in practice. As might have been expected, the divorce rate rose. But after the divorce the ex-wife, instead of being free, was usually saddled with the children; she had to care for them, while the man, bound by no law, could go off, "happily whistling." Middle-aged women complained that their husbands were taking advantage of the liberal laws to desert them for younger women. According to one critic, freedom of divorce, instead of emancipating women, "turned out in fact to be a man's policy. It provided Soviet husbands with ideological and legal support for sexual adventure, but abandoned their wives to *de facto* exploitation."

In addition, the children of broken homes were often left on their own, a state of things that contributed to the severe juvenile delinquency that plagued Russia during the turbulent 1920's and into the 1930's. Even the children of dedicated Communists were running amok. One observer wrote: "In certain cases, the parents of young delinquents were giving all their time to the community, and neglecting their children."

If this weren't enough, the nation's birth rate began to fall—a worrisome matter to official planners who were counting on a large work force to man the fields and the factories and, as war threatened in the 1930's, to enter the army. "We have need of people," declared Soviet officials.

To sum up, as one writer has: "In the absence of substitute institutions, the obstacles placed in the path of traditional patterns of family life created an atmosphere of disorganization and uncertainty."

In the 1930's, Communist planners, whose principles had not been working at all well in practice, began an extraordinary turnabout in their attitude toward the family. Now divorce, abortion, and sexual freedom were denounced and the family was praised in official propaganda. "Marriage is the most serious affair in life," announced the party newspaper *Pravda* in 1936, when reforms were made in the Family Code. "Fatherhood and motherhood become virtues in the Soviet land." Husbands were warned that, to be good citizens, they first had to be good family men.

The official line was set down by a professor of law: "Marriage, basically and in the spirit of Soviet law, is in principle a lifelong union. Moreover, marriage receives its full value for the Soviet state only if there is birth of children, proper upbringing, and if the spouses experience the highest happiness of motherhood and fatherhood." The new line was highly unrevolutionary, highly conventional. In less than a decade, the regime's policies toward the family had been utterly transformed. A historian writes: "Responsibility and reproduction were the order of the day; stable marriages, large families, and self-discipline were now more important to the regime than individual freedom, sex equality, and ideological consistency." Now parents were entrusted with the duty of raising their children to be patriotic, hard-working, true to party regulations, and so forth: "The main importance of the family comes from its work of preparing the new generation for Communism."

Women's chores in the household, which the early Communist leaders had derided, were now praised as socially useful labor. The Soviet newspaper *Izvestia* wrote: "Though boys and girls must have access to all professions and should be trained for them, girls must be educated to be loving and capable mothers and rearers of children, and schools for girls must also develop femininity, modesty, and a sense of the great worthiness and honor of women." The movement toward co-education, girls and boys attending classes together, was reversed.

Now children were instructed to love and respect their parents. Only registered marriages were legally binding; the wedding ceremony, which early Communists had laughed at, once again received official sanction. Divorce, on the other hand, was penalized—at first mildly, and then so severely that it became almost impossible for most people. In August 1944, a month after the announcement of major new family laws, not a single petition for divorce was filed in the entire country.

Because of the falling birth rate, abortions were made illegal. Bachelors and couples with fewer than three children were subject to steep fines, whereas mothers of large families received cash allowances, medals, and assorted honors. Having seven children rated an Order of the Glory of Motherhood medal, third class. The bearer of ten children became a Mother Heroine.

Under the dictatorship of Joseph Stalin, the chief Soviet virtues became discipline, allegiance to the regime, and subordination of the individual to the state. The early Communist dream of liberating individuals from antiquated and restrictive ties was replaced by a view of the family as an instrument of the state in bringing up obedient, hard-working citizens who would perform their assigned tasks and never become troublemakers. It was, of course, precisely this use of the family by Czarist authorities and the Russian Orthodox Church that had aroused the indignation of the early revolutionists.

Since the end of World War II, Soviet society has undergone many changes, including technical advances and improvements in living standards which have permitted a relaxation of the laws on family life. Divorces are easier to get; abortions are permissible under certain circumstances; taxes on the childless have been eliminated. A shortage of child-care facilities still prevents women from getting out of the home and into the work force, however. As one woman wrote not long ago in a letter to the newspaper *Pravda:* "The school attended by my daughter was on three sessions. There was no lunchroom or after-school program. I had to quit work because you can't leave children without supervision. Now the girl is older, but I have a baby. Here's a new worry. How shall I arrange for a nursery for her?"

The experience of the Soviet Union's early years tells us a good deal about the nature of dictatorship as well as about the nature of the family. In attempting first to destroy the family and later to make it a servant of the state, the Soviet regime interfered grossly in the private affairs of its citizens. Individual desires were subordinated to the state's requirements. According to a Soviet newspaper, "A Soviet person cannot simply love someone, without political or moral watchfulness. Our Soviet citizen can no longer love only because of a natural drive. He wants his beloved to be worthy of his feeling, to possess the best Soviet qualities."

Ironically, the Russian people, bound to age-old ways, seemed to take more naturally to the repressive rules of Stalin than to the efforts at liberation introduced by the early

Communist theorists. As for these early efforts, one observer writes: "In Russia, the notion that family institutions and organizations are merely bourgeois arrangements, unnecessary for the maintenance of a Socialist society and its citizens, has been totally discredited if not disproved."

The Soviet planners found that although the family can be changed and made to adapt to new requirements and new social arrangements, it cannot be destroyed by the passage of a few laws. Against the great powers of a totalitarian state, the family showed remarkable staying power.

*

The type of agricultural settlement known as the *kibbutz,* developed by the Jewish pioneers in the land that would become Israel, was revolutionary in a number of respects. We shall focus here on the changes it brought about in the traditional Jewish habits and ideals of family life.

The family was at the center of the society created by the millions of Jews who lived in Eastern Europe in the early decades of the twentieth century. The family was a refuge for these people who were often harshly discriminated against and excluded from many political, economic, and social activities.

In the traditional Jewish family, there was complete separation between the responsibilities and routines of men and women—a total division of labor. The man had the duty of providing food, clothing, and shelter for his wife and children. The woman had the duty of running the household. Men were all-powerful in the synagogue; women were all-powerful in the kitchen. Whereas a son would be given years of religious training, a daughter's lessons would be centered on housekeeping. Marriages were arranged by parents for their children, with an eye toward economic security, and grandchildren became a treasured part of the family group.

This model was not at all to the taste of the young Jews who began settling in Palestine in growing numbers soon after World War I. For the most part, they went there on their own, without parents or relatives. They had broken away from their families and were in revolt against prevailing economic and social conditions. Many were socialists; they believed in people working together for the benefit of the whole community rather than for this household or that, and they saw in the untamed land of Palestine an opportunity to turn their ideals into reality. They considered themselves emancipated from religious dogma, and they rejected life as it had to be lived in the besieged Jewish enclaves of Eastern Europe. At the same time that they were eager to give their labor and their loyalty to their new society, they aspired to a kind of freedom that was not available to Jews in the countries from which many of them came.

Moreover, the nature of the land they were settling called for a very different style of life from the small-town style of Eastern Europe. The new settlers arrived to find themselves in a desert, an uncultivated and alien place which it was up to them to cultivate and defend. It was an enormously difficult job, and their only hope of success was to pool their strength and their skills for the good of all. The *kibbutz* had to be a combination farm, school, and military outpost. Like the American pioneer settlement, it was close-knit and self-sustaining, designed to meet the needs of all its inhabitants, from the youngest to the oldest. The combination of needs and ideals produced a way of living that would have shocked the new settlers' forebears.

As we examine the changes in family life wrought by the nature of the *kibbutz,* we should keep in mind, first, that most Israelis do not live on such communal settlements and, second, that the *kibbutzim* differ in many respects among themselves. We shall concentrate on those that broke most sharply with the concepts of family life practiced and valued highly by most of Europe's Jews.

One big goal in the *kibbutzim* was absolute equality between men and women. No longer would there be a "head of the family." No longer would women be subordinated to men, as they had been in Europe. Instead of the man going forth each day to earn a living for his family, everyone, women and men alike, would pitch in and do the work that had to be done to make the land fruitful and the community safe. Women and men would play an equal role in the governing of the *kibbutz*.

Instead of a woman minding her own house and her own children, housekeeping would be done on a community-wide basis. Meals would be prepared in a communal kitchen and served in a communal dining hall. Children would be raised in nurseries and dormitories. To make sure that personal relationships did not get in the way of communal duties, members of a family were forbidden to work in the same place. Husbands and wives would not even coordinate their vacations and days off, because the needs of the group took precedence over the desires of individuals.

Instead of each husband working for his mate and each family striving to accumulate the most it could in the way of physical goods, the proceeds of all labor would go into a communal fund, and the commune's members would share goods and services, in accord with the socialist dictum: *From each according to his ability; to each according to his need.* So the family would no longer be the basic economic unit. There would be a small cash allowance for each person. Such private possessions as radios and electric kettles were banned at first in some communes, for fear that they would make the individual dwelling too attractive and so discourage people from participating fully in *kibbutz* affairs.

Instead of marriages being carefully negotiated and

strictly arranged by elders, mating was to be an entirely personal matter. Two people who decided to join their lives would simply ask the *kibbutz* housing committee for a room together—and that was that. They would continue to work at whatever jobs they had worked at before. The marriage ceremony would be a mere formality, sometimes performed only to make a newborn child legitimate under the law of the land. The wife would retain her maiden name.

A student of *kibbutz* life has shown how the young settlers' attitudes toward marriage were reflected in the words they used to talk about it: "From the very beginning, the terms 'marriage,' 'husband,' 'wife,' were abandoned because of their invidious connotations. A man and a woman do not get 'married'; they become a 'pair.' A woman does not acquire a 'husband'; she acquires a 'young man' or a 'companion.' By the same token, a man acquires not a 'wife,' but a 'young woman' or a 'companion.' "

Under such conditions, many decisions which had formerly been left to the family group now became a matter for the entire community—the job one held, the place one lived and the way it was furnished, the meals one ate and where one ate them, the vacations one took. As an observer put it, "In effect, the *kibbutz* as a whole acts as a 'great family' for all its members."

The point was understood by the *kibbutz* child who asked his father: "Who told you to make me a boy?" When the father did not come up with an acceptable answer, the child said: "I know, it must have been on the daily work sheet."

Let's look a bit more closely at the way a *kibbutz* might actually go about separating parents and offspring, taking over the family role in such critical matters as raising children and selecting mates.

Children have always held a precious place in Jewish life,

and the *kibbutz* carries on that tradition—but with major innovations. Soon after a baby is born, it is placed in the Infants' House, or nursery, while its mother remains at home for a week or so, convalescing. Except for nursing visits by the mother, the baby is cared for by women whose full-time job is to work in the nursery. By the time the child is weaned, the mother is back at her own full-time job elsewhere on the *kibbutz.* "The emancipation of woman," one *kibbutznik* has said, "depends on whether she is relieved of the burden of looking after children in the evening."

As the child grows and is moved from the Infants' House to the Toddlers' House, he or she will have nightly visits of about two hours with the parents, but the responsibility for training and discipline rests with the *kibbutz* specialists in child care. It is these specialists who feed, bathe, and dress the youngsters, and tend them when they are ill.

Between the time a child is about five years old until high school, he or she lives with other children of like age. A child eats, sleeps, and plays, not in the home of his parents, but with this group in their own mini-commune. Here, from the very beginnings of life into the teens, the center of social existence is a community of peers. The peer group, not the family, is the focus of the child's world. During the whole growing-up time, however, daily visits between parents and children are common, and family feelings are nurtured.

After high school, dormitory life ends. The young woman or man, who has already been working part-time outside school hours, becomes a full-fledged *kibbutznik,* with a job and a room of his or her own. This is an age for romance, of course, but the experience has been that young people who have grown up together in such close quarters tend to think of the other boys and girls on their *kibbutz* as brothers and sisters, and look elsewhere for mates, often in other *kibbutzim.* A sociologist who lived among these young people reports: "We have not come across even one love affair or one instance of publicly known sexual relations between members of the same peer group who were co-socialized from birth on through most of their childhood."

The picture, then, as far as our ordinary notions of the family are concerned, is of a society where a great many of the functions that we ordinarily think of as belonging to a mother and father are taken over by the larger group. The family remains—but in a decidedly weakened form.

What has been happening to the *kibbutz* principles and the *kibbutz* families in the thirty years since Israel has been a state? Life has become easier and more secure (at least on a day-to-day basis), and the early settlers' zeal has been modified with the passage of time. Instead of being solitary, largely male outposts in an alien land, the settlements are now part of a thriving country, in close touch with towns, cities, and other settlements.

The residents of the *kibbutzim* are older, with families of their own. Many of the early ideals are still held, but the role of the family has been altered in response to changed conditions and pressures from individual members. The *kibbutz* is still of great importance to its inhabitants—but by no means to the exclusion of the family. In a number of ways, as a matter of fact, the family is impinging on what was once assumed to be the prerogatives of the community as a whole. Some of the changes have been graphically conveyed in a report published in *The New York Times:*

"The image of the *kibbutz* women, sunburned and standing guard against infiltrating Arabs, is largely a product of Zionist propagandists. Actually, the women are as housebound as ordinary wives, except that they are confined to the kitchens and laundries of the community, not of their own homes.

"It was largely the rebellious women who forced the

changes that have already taken hold in the *kibbutzim*. The mothers are gaining increasing responsibility for the care of their own children. The apartments are being increasingly furnished with radios, paintings, individual wardrobes and electric kettles for brewing tea and coffee at home."

A typical dwelling these days is a semi-detached apartment with one or two rooms, a kitchenette, and a private bathroom. The apartments have grown more attractive as families have taken greater pains in decorating them and putting in extra gadgets. The rising standard of living has led to more conspicuous expressions of private consumption. A great portion of people's allowances appears to be going for such personal items as clothing and cosmetics; women are trying to look more "feminine."

Nowadays, husbands and wives spend much of their time together at home, and usually take care to sit beside each other during evening meals and at meetings and entertainments as well. Indeed, entertaining has become something of a family affair; it is considered impolite to invite a husband somewhere without inviting his wife too. Relatives now tend to cluster together within villages; the wider kinship ties that were broken in the early days of the *kibbutz* are being reestablished. Family members try to get together whenever the occasion permits. On holidays, relatives journey miles to see one another. Vacation schedules are arranged to permit husbands and wives to have the same periods free. In some places, families gather privately for their evening meals.

Observers have noticed an increased use of the words "wife" and "husband," which were avoided in the early *kibbutz* days, and children call their parents "mother" and "father." Marriage has become an important ceremony, with the wife generally taking her husband's name instead of keeping her maiden name. The birth rate has gone up; people are more eager to have children.

While the children are growing, parents take a more active part in looking after them—watching over them at night, nursing them when they are ill, supervising their behavior, helping to organize their games, and simply playing with them. One woman expressed a widely held feeling among *kibbutz* mothers: "They bring up all sorts of arguments and evidence, but I am clear about one thing—I miss my child and want him with me, and that's all there is to it." Even in the early days, many parents would start their work at sunrise in order to have more time to spend with their young children in the afternoon, and today women show a preference for working close to the children's houses. They are voluntarily doing "women's work" in the laundries and kitchens, rather than laboring in the fields.

So on the Israeli *kibbutz,* as in the U.S.S.R., the nature of the family has been changed to conform to revolutionary ideals and the needs of a new society. But in both places the strength of the family proved itself, as people insisted on what seem to be elemental human desires for an intimate relationship with one's mate and with one's children, a special relationship that can be kept separate from the rest of the community.

These experiences can only enhance our appreciation of the power of the family to endure over the ages in many different, often uncongenial social and political settings.

III

THE

AMERICAN

FAMILY

FIVE

The American Family: Yesterday

The colonial period is a reasonable place to start if we are trying to understand the transformations of family life in the centuries since the European settlement of America. The place the family held among the Pilgrims grew out of a combination of their history in the old world of England and the demands of the new world of New England. They were Puritans who had broken with the Established Church in their native land. They held to very strict standards of sexual behavior and an unequivocal view of the proper relationship among husbands, wives, and children. The husband was to be master of the household, the wife was to be faithful, the children were to be obedient.

The Pilgrims were accustomed to struggling for their livelihood. They were a hard-working, no-nonsense sort of people—which was fortunate, given the hardships that they had to endure and overcome after their arrival on these shores.

The members of the colonial farm family were all producers; everyone capable of working worked, either on the farm or in the household. Children were treated like small adults. Boys followed their father's lead; girls assisted their mother with the cooking, cleaning, sewing. From the earliest years, they were prepared to run households of their own.

Every farm family had to make virtually all its own goods —furniture, clothes, shoes, soap, candles, and so forth. Every home was a miniature factory, with all its members in a kind of partnership. Every housewife had to be a combination doctor and druggist, not only able to prescribe and administer drugs for all manner of illnesses, but also able to compound them out of available herbs. It is difficult for most of us today to appreciate the painstaking, muscle-straining, time-consuming efforts that went into the making, day after day, of items that we pick up as a matter of course at the supermarket. Everything, remember, had to be done by hand, from obtaining the raw materials to storing the final product.

Here, to take a relatively simple example, is a description of how candles were made each fall in preparation for the winter months: "Two huge kettles half-filled with boiling water and melted tallow, which had already been scalded and twice skimmed, were hung in the open fireplace. In a cooler place, small sticks called 'candle rods' were placed across two long poles. About six or eight straightened candle wicks were attached to each candle rod, and then each rod was dipped into the melted tallow and hung up to cool and harden. This was repeated so that the candles steadily grew until the right size was obtained. Two hundred candles could be made in a day if the workers were good and the room fairly cool so that the tallow hardened quickly."

If we, dependent as we are on electric light switches and instant brightness at all hours and in all seasons, consider that this was but one, and not the most complicated or arduous, of the colonial family's innumerable tasks, we may begin to sense the degree to which the family's existence was centered on basic chores. After the colonial period, too, as families moved West to settle the new lands on the American frontier, there was never a shortage of chores to go around, though sometimes there was a shortage of hands to do them. The work was endless and back-breaking.

In view of the many jobs that needed doing in the New England colonies, it is no wonder that men were on the lookout for wives who were skilled, thrifty and, above all, hard-working. (They were not expected to be educated.) A girl needed a husband for support, since there was scarcely any work open to her outside the house. The few women who remained without husbands in colonial days were looked down on—it was agreed that something must be the matter with them—and parents were likely to be embarrassed to have an unwed daughter on their hands. Unmarried women of twenty-five were described as a "dismal spectacle."

Unmarried men were not in much better repute. In Hartford, bachelors were taxed twenty shillings a week "for the selfish luxury of solitary living." They were expected to report periodically to a magistrate just to make sure they were behaving themselves. Puritan New England did not look kindly upon young marriageable males whiling away their time when they could be producing children. This was no place for sowing wild oats.

The mortality rate was high in those early days, and there were never enough hands to do the jobs that needed doing. People were expected to marry early and have big families. There are reports of twenty children and more in a family. Cotton Mather, the powerful New England clergyman, set an example by having sixteen children—and outliving all but one of them.

If the husband or the wife died, the surviving spouse was expected to marry again promptly. One Isaac Winslow may have carried this custom to an unreasonable extreme when he proposed to a girl just a few hours after he buried his first wife. The first marriage recorded in Plymouth was between a man who had been widowed for seven weeks and a woman who had been widowed for twelve weeks. Living alone in a small, rather narrow-minded town where everyone knew everyone else was no pleasure in early New England.

It was accepted among the Puritans that sex was to be confined to marriage, and within marriage, the purpose of sex was the conceiving of children. Young New Englanders had more freedom in selecting a mate than young Europeans did, but since the family was primarily an economic unit, men usually expected substantial dowries to come along with their brides, and there was much haggling over marriage settlements. It was a case of business before pleasure. The newly married woman became in effect a ward of her husband. All her property, including her clothing and jewelry, was his to do with as he saw fit.

Still, romance was not altogether absent even among these practical-minded people. There was, for example, the celebrated custom of "bundling." When a young fellow came courting on a cold winter's night, instead of wasting candlelight and firewood, he and the girl he had come to pay his respects to would retire under the bedcovers, without removing their clothing, and continue their conversation. It is said that most of the young folks did nothing more intimate there in the dark, under the quilt, than converse.

In the colonial household, the man was very much in charge. In every Puritan home there was one chair set aside for the father's use; it symbolized his authority. His discipline tended to be severe. Children had to pay attention to their chores and to their religious instruction; if their attention wandered or if they themselves went wandering when needed at work, punishment followed. Here is a portion of a book of table etiquette for children in colonial New England: "Never sit down at table till asked, and after the blessing. Ask for nothing; tarry till it be offered thee. Speak not, hum not, wriggle not . . ."

To sum up: the family was the indispensable unit of colonial life. Everybody belonged to a family and every family operated as a workshop, a school, a place of worship, and a place of recreation. The rules under which it operated may seem strict to us today, but it was those rules and the tight family groupings which they supported that helped the early New Englanders to survive extremely difficult and dangerous conditions. Their example influenced and helped to sustain the frontier families of the nineteenth century, who were confronted by similar hardships.

*

There was, of course, more to early America than New England and New Englanders. In the South, where the climate was more benign and settlers tended to be more easygoing than New England's Puritans, a form of chivalry arose among the upper-class plantation owners toward their women. It was a combination of adulation, deference, protection, and condescension. The plantation male, imitating an aristocratic model not esteemed in New England, was bound to see to it that his lady was not harmed or embarrassed or put into disagreeable situations; on the other hand, women were on no account supposed to impinge on male prerogatives.

The Southern girl was no better educated and had no more economic rights than the New England girl. Whereas upper-class girls were expected to be chaste, boys were expected to be promiscuous—with lower-class white girls and, occasionally, with black female slaves. A seventeenth-century book called on women to be meek, modest, affable, compassionate, and pious.

Like the New England family, the Southern family was the center of its members' lives. Distances between plantations were long, and roads were not good—a situation which may have led to the development of the fabled Southern hospitality. People were delighted to visit and to receive visitors who brought news from afar and offered an excuse for enlivening the family routine.

The Southern family produced most of what it needed and, as in New England, provided for its own schooling, worship, and recreation. In poor families, naturally, there was less time or inclination for schooling, worship, and recreation; everybody worked, and worked hard. Among wealthier families, as the plantation system developed, the bulk of the physical labor came to be performed by slaves.

*

The impact of slavery on the family life of America's black population has become a matter of heated controversy in recent years. For a century it was accepted by most historians that many or most slaves were prevented from setting up enduring families of their own.

Basing their conclusions largely on the writings of pre-Civil War abolitionists and the recollections of former slaves, historians reported that on many plantations slave women were encouraged to breed—so that their children might be sold at auction. Some planters, they wrote, encouraged promiscuity among slaves; a girl was induced to begin bearing children early, often by a variety of partners, and to keep producing them until she was no longer physically able to give birth. The historians tended to agree that attractive slave girls were subject to the attentions of the white master and his sons, and that the mulatto children of such unions became slaves without fathers.

The cruelest shock to the slave family came when one or another of its members was sold at auction. Here is a widely quoted description of such a sale by a former slave: "The first sad announcement that the sale was to be; the knowledge that all ties of the past are to be sundered; the frantic terror of being sent 'down south'; the almost certainty that one member of the family will be torn from another; the anxious scanning of purchasers' faces; the agony at parting, often forever, with husband, wife, child—these must be seen and felt to be fully understood. Young as I was then, the iron entered my soul."

Such cruelties did undoubtedly take place. However, recent findings by historians using advanced statistical techniques give us quite a different picture of the slave family than the one painted by the abolitionists. Black families appear to have been of central importance on the plantation, and efforts were made to keep them together. The slave family was in most cases headed by the husband and encouraged and respected by the plantation owner. Sexual promiscuity was not the rule. Slave life pivoted around stable black families.

How the dispute among historians will turn out, we cannot say. At the very least, it does appear that plantation owners recognized some benefit to their own interests in encouraging marriage among their slaves. One former slave recalled:

Marsa used to sometimes pick our wives fo' us. If he didn't have on his place enough women for the men, he would wait on de side of de road till a big wagon loaded with slaves come by. Den Marsa would stop de ole nigger-trader and buy you a woman. Wasn't no use tryin' to pick one, cause Marsa wasn't gonna pay but so much for her. All he wanted was a healthy one who looked like she could have children, whether she was purty or ugly as sin. Den he would lead you an' de woman over to one of de cabins and stan' you dere at de do' and open de Bible to de first thing he come to an' read somepin' real fast out of it. Den he close up de Bible an' finish up wid dis verse:

> *Dat you' wife*
> *Dat you' husban'.*
> *I's you' Marsa*
> *She you' Missus.*
> *You married.*

In some places, the law worked against efforts to maintain stable black families. The North Carolina Supreme Court ruled: "The relation between slaves is essentially different from that of man and wife joined in lawful wedlock." The court pointed out that a marriage of two slaves could be "dissolved at the pleasure of either party, or by the sale of one or both, depending upon the caprice or the necessity of the owner."

On the other hand, some owners were acutely sensitive to the sufferings caused by the breaking up of black families—like the woman in Virginia who freed her slaves in her will rather than subject them to possible sale by her heirs, because "I cannot satisfy my conscience to have my Negro slaves separated from each other and from their husbands and wives." Many owners took pains to sell their slaves only in family groups, and only to buyers in the same part of the country, who pledged to keep the families intact. There were also numerous instances of planters purchasing a worker's wife or husband from another plantation so that man and wife could be together. Few owners appear to have been as brutal as the plantation manager who, asked by a Northern visitor about children being separated from their mothers, explained: "These Negroes do not feel these things as we do. They are an altogether inferior race of beings and have no strong affections."

The shattering of the system of slavery by the Civil War, the trauma of Emancipation, and the discrimination against black people which has stained American life in the past century have had devastating effects on black family life. In big-city ghettos today, the bitter heritage of slavery combined with continuing economic deprivation has resulted in a weak family structure—the father often absent, the mother working, the children left on their own without a strong male figure in the house.

As young black men and women enter the middle class in substantial numbers, their family lives are being strengthened along with their strengthened economic status. That is not true of another group which has suffered grievously at the hands of white America. Indians have not sought to follow the American pattern—nor have they been welcome to follow it. They have attempted to maintain tribal arrangements which are ill suited to our economic and political system. They are faced now with the painful choice of trying to become part of that system and so raise their low standard of living at the expense of giving up precious traditions and a valued way of life, or holding to their tribal ways and remaining on the outskirts of American society.

*

As Americans moved West after the Revolution, their family patterns were influenced by the colonial experience, by the traditions of the European lands from which most of them came, and by the nature and location of the new areas where they settled.

Frontier families were generally large, as families tend to be where labor is needed. As in New England, the home was the center of life, for both work and play. Everybody pitched in, and the father was in charge.

However, the Westerners were not Puritans; their lands proved easier to cultivate than the rocky soil of New England; and frontier living, with its vast spaces and with isolated groups of people dependent on each other for survival, seemed to encourage more leeway in personal relations. A rough sort of democracy seemed natural out West, and it made its effects felt within the family, especially as the harsh, perilous conditions that faced the early settlers eased somewhat.

Although the large, hard-working farm family was bound together by common economic needs, the bonds were more flexible than among the Pilgrims. Family life was not as rigid. There was just as much mutual allegiance among family members, with less repression. Religious practices in the West were not nearly as strict as in early New England; numerous denominations established themselves and none had the power or the inclinations of the Puritan clergy. The young were allowed greater freedom, women were not in quite so subservient a position. The early American farm family was more democratic than anything that had come before, a part of the emerging democratic style in America.

Instead of judging the value of the family by how well it performed in the interests of a clan or tribe or the society as a whole, Americans on the frontier tended to see it in terms of its members. Individuality and independence early became part of the American faith. One observer writes: "Individual achievement, development, or happiness is, in implicit American tradition, the desired end; the family is regarded by the country, and by the individual, as a private venture for the sake of personal satisfaction." The spirit is: "One for all and all for one"—with heavy emphasis on the second part of that motto.

The picture left to us of those frontier and farm times is of whopping-big breakfasts, with old folks and babies and everybody in-between gathered together around a laden board. This is an unrealistically idyllic scene, no doubt; yet it does convey something of the warmth that pervaded the old-style farm household, and the image continues to exert a powerful appeal in present-day America.

But the country was changing fast in the nineteenth century, and within a few generations, as we shall see in the next chapter, the large farm unit would be displaced as the typical American family.

SIX

The American Family: Today

In chapter 3, we noted the impact of the industrial revolution on the European family. Nowhere has large-scale industry taken firmer hold than in the United States; the consequences for our lives, in particular our family lives, have been incalculable. One great change, with many ramifications, has been the shift from the *extended* family to the *nuclear* family.

*

A family grouping that consists of more than two parents and their children is considered an *extended* family. Not so long ago, for example, it was common for grandparents, parents, and children to make their home together. These three-generation households were typical on the frontier and on farms in America's heartland. They still exist in reduced numbers in many parts of this country, and they still exist in our collective memory—as indicated by the recent success of television shows featuring families in which children, adults, and elderly people share daily experiences. The classic extended family is the traditional Chinese family, where a husband and wife live in one household, along with the families of their married sons as well as with their unmarried sons and daughters. Another kind of extended or *joint* family, found among some Indian tribes, brings together groups of brothers and their wives to work as a team on the family lands.

For people living in rural areas, we have already seen, the extended family makes a lot of sense. Everyone pitches in and works; everyone shares in the fruits of the labor; everyone knows that in time of trouble there will be a place to sleep, food to eat, and kin nearby to provide comfort and security.

The extended family is still able to hold the loyalties of its members. When men from the poor rural Appalachia region of eastern Kentucky are forced to leave home to seek jobs in cities in Ohio, they tend to stick together in their new settings, and to keep a connection to those whom they have left behind. This arrangement is sometimes called the *stem* family. That is, the parent household back in Appalachia can be considered the stem of a tree. Usually one grown son remains in the family homestead, which cannot support more than a few people; the others go off to earn their living elsewhere. The brothers who leave are the branches of the tree. If they prosper in the big city, they can send some cash back home; if they find themselves in difficulty, they will always have a shelter they can return to and kin who can be counted on to help them out. As long as these connections are maintained, family traditions can be preserved.

The stem family was part of the feudal system as it existed in medieval Europe and in Japan from the beginning of the seventeenth to the middle of the nineteenth century. The Japanese household was entrusted to the oldest son, who was thereafter responsible for preserving its traditions and paying reverence to his ancestors.

Another effort to maintain an extended family system in twentieth-century America can be seen among the Amish of Pennsylvania. Recognizing that our modern economic setup is incompatible with extended family groups, the Amish have in effect cut themselves off from contemporary society. They earn their living mainly as farmers and operate under stringent self-imposed rules that cover the types of work they do, their manner of dress, the limits they place on the education of their young, and much else. They are aware of the temptations of the outside world, and by insulating themselves, they have been able so far to retain some of the strengths of the old-style rural family.

Other examples of extended families, sustained as much by circumstances as by choice, can be found around the country. In remote areas of Tennessee, for example, kinship groups related by blood continue to be forceful agencies of self-government. We still hear of feuds between two such clans as they take the law into their own hands to settle disputes with shooting irons. Such feuds, accurately called "blood feuds," resemble a kind of tribal warfare. The mountain people have refused to give up to the official police force the kinship group's valued role as protector of its own, and they will defy the police in defense of one of their members who has run afoul of the law.

In our urban ghettos, we can find many extended households headed by females, where grandmother, mother, and children live together. The children's father may be gone, or he may appear from time to time, but the daily operations of the family are in the hands of the adult women.

*

The foregoing examples are all exceptions to the rule in America today. The rule is the *nuclear* family—consisting typically of a married man and woman and their children. (The nucleus of anything is its central part, as the father-mother-child group is the central part of the extended family.) The nuclear family is a relationship based on biology, not on blood. Wife and husband are united, not by any requirements of a larger kinship group, but by their mutual needs and by their children.

We have already reviewed the reasons why the nuclear family took hold in an industrial society, the reasons why a basic grouping of father, mother, and children is more suited to present-day urban society than the other family arrangements we have discussed. It has to do, remember, with the fact that in our big cities one member of the family, usually the father, is the breadwinner and the rest of the family depends on him for support; with the fact that people are no longer tied to the land but can and must move around to get the best jobs possible; with the fact that space is more precious in the city than in the country; and with the fact that the government, in one form or another, has taken on many of the functions that the extended farm family used to provide pretty much on its own. In brief, the kinship group has become far less important to individual members than it was in a pre-industrial age.

Now let's look in a bit more detail at the effects of these changes on the middle-class family in America. (Both the wealthiest and the poorest portions of the population tend to alter their family patterns more slowly than the middle class; both are more resistant to social change.)

For one thing, power in the nuclear family (nuclear

power?) tends to be more diffused. There is no patriarch to whom all members of the family must pay homage. Nowadays, a child's grandfather is likely to have little direct control over his grandchildren's or even his own grown children's lives; more often than not, he is a benevolent figure who visits, with gifts for the kiddies, or is visited on festive occasions or as a kind of routine duty.

The father of the family would seem to have the lion's share of economic power, since, in the typical situation, he is the one who goes forth each day to earn the family's living. But his use of that power is to a great degree regulated by the state; he can't spend the money as he might wish; he is obligated by law to support his wife and children. Moreover, since it is the wife who does most of the family spending on a daily basis, she has substantial economic power of her own. (TV commercials are directed much more at women than at men, except for such high-priced items as automobiles.)

The upbringing of young children is generally left to the wife, since she is with them all day while her husband is away. But at the age of five, or even earlier, the children go off to school, and teachers and principals begin to play an important part in their development.

It takes a boy or girl many more years to begin working full-time than it used to, but by the late teens or early twenties most people are physically capable of getting jobs and beginning life apart from their families. They may, of course, be bound to parents, brothers, and sisters by strong emotions and memories, but there is usually no family work for them to share and most youths today do not follow in their father's footsteps when choosing a trade or profession. Since the family is no longer a unit of production, there is no gainful employment for the young around the house. Unless they come from very wealthy homes, they have little choice after a certain point but to go out and try to get along on their own.

Along with a portion of economic independence for young people goes more freedom in selecting a mate than was generally available in a patriarchal setup. As we have indicated, the main parties to a marriage used to be the parents of the bride and groom. Two families were being joined, and questions of wealth and status took precedence over the desires of the young pair. Today men and women in their twenties have considerable latitude in choosing their marriage partners—even though their selections are still subject to parental influence as well as to considerations of wealth and social position.

Not only is there more leeway in entering marriage, there is more leeway in leaving it, or in avoiding it altogether. We have seen that in colonial times a stigma was attached to unmarried women and men. By and large, that is no longer the case. Today there are no pressing economic reasons for a young man to marry; he has no need of a family to help with the farm chores. As for the young woman, she may still find it difficult to make a career for herself outside the home and she is likely to be under social pressures to find a husband, but women, too, are in a better position to get along unmarried than they have ever been before.

As for the sexual pleasures of marriage, these are increasingly available to both men and women without the ceremony, the vows, the ring. Though religious spokesmen may decry the situation, the fact remains that people can and do find satisfying sexual relationships outside of marriage. Moreover, there have been recent court rulings to the effect that a child born out of wedlock is entitled to share in the father's estate. Since one of the main functions of the family has traditionally been to establish a child's legitimacy for purposes of inheritance, such rulings serve further to reduce the family's significance.

Other important functions once assigned to the family have also been taken away.

Children once received most of their education at home. Now they must leave the house at an early age and go out to a school run by the state or a church or private educators. School days and years are longer than they used to be, which means more time spent away from the household.

Once a child's activities were the exclusive concern of the family; now there are child labor laws and juvenile courts which impinge on parents' prerogatives.

Old people once depended on their sons and daughters for support. Now, though family contributions are still significant, the government provides Social Security payments, Medicaid, and other aids to the elderly, which serve to reduce their dependence on their families and increase their dependence on the state.

The medical, police, and safety functions once reserved to the family have been largely taken over by official agencies or departments. People don't have to put out their own fires any more.

Once recreation was mainly a household affair; now people find their recreation outside the house, mostly with friends of their own age rather than with members of the family. (It seemed for a time that TV-watching might again unite families—but then households began getting two or more sets so that parents and offspring could watch different shows in different rooms.)

Once religion was part of a family's daily life. Today a family may go to church together once a week—or it may not make even that gesture to organized religion. In any case, for many people, religious worship has become a social rather than a family matter.

So today's nuclear family has been divested of many of the roles which the family once had in this country. Along with a reduction in its usefulness has gone a reduction in its power over the lives of its members, since individuals have much less to lose today than they once did if they rebel against family conventions. But let's resist jumping to the conclusion that the family has hardly any functions left at all. That is far from the case. There are four vital areas, always associated with family life, in which the present-day family continues to play a significant part.

Sex. Despite the degree of sexual liberty available today, the family continues to be the means whereby the vast majority of men and women find a sexual outlet and the instrument which society uses to exercise a degree of control over sexual activity.

Reproduction and rearing. It is within a family structure that people continue to have children and care for them in the years when they are helpless. The state still depends on the family to insure the well-being of infants and small children. Officials enter into it only when the family seems to be failing in its responsibilities.

Education and socialization. Although schools have pretty much taken over from the home the job of imparting skills and information, most children's formative years are still spent largely within the family group. Educators acknowledge the vital impact of these early years on the child's future potential for schooling. Moreover, it is in the home rather than in the classroom that children develop their most basic values and outlook. Experiences at home still play a crucial role in determining the sort of people they will grow up to be.

Economics. For all the progress in opening up new career possibilities to women, most married couples still find that the specialization of labor within the nuclear family suits their requirements. The man goes off to his factory or office to earn the family's living. The wife stays home to watch over the children and the house, perhaps to take part in community activities. The nuclear family is a perfect setting for this division of responsibilities.

To sum up: although the nuclear family has fewer tasks assigned to it than the extended family had, the tasks it does undertake are still significant. The family continues to have its specialized role among all the specialized institutions of contemporary society. Whether this role is in the main beneficial to people and to the society or harmful remains a source of continuing dispute.

Let's look at some of the pros and cons.

*

Most critics seem agreed that the basic weakness of the nuclear family, particularly as it exists in the United States, is its isolation. Every newly married couple starts afresh. The household is neither patrilocal nor matrilocal; when two people marry, they generally go off and set up an independent household, away from both sets of parents. This household is *neolocal,* established in a new location. Quite often, job requirements take the couple many miles away from their former homes. Whereas once most people were likely to die near the spot where they were born, many young families in America nowadays change their dwelling places numerous times to meet the career needs of the husband.

Whereas in other times marriages were arranged by families which were acquainted with each other and shared common values, today's bride and groom are likely to come from families which would never have met except for the accident of a girl and a boy falling in love. Dating is pretty much a twentieth-century phenomenon, made possible by the transfer of boys and girls from the labor force into high schools and colleges.

Sometimes, to be sure, childhood sweethearts do get married, even today, and there are ethnic groups, such as the Amish or the ultra-Orthodox Jews known as Hasidim, who strive to insulate their young from outside contacts—but such enclaves encounter great difficulties in maintaining a cherished way of life. Increasingly, young people from quite different backgrounds meet on campuses, in offices, at dances; they court without much regard for family tradition; they are preparing to break off from their own small family groups.

(We should add that, even with the unprecedented breadth of choice that young people have today, an important part is still played by religion, social class, ethnic background, education, and geography in bringing potential partners together. As a sociologist has observed about courtship in America: "While romantic self-choice is the basis of marriage, there are actually many hedges upon the unrestrained exercise of it. Love has a habit of enkindling two persons ordinarily when, by social rules, they are eligible or it is wise that they marry each other; beyond prescribed limits, intransigent love is usually snuffed out. Like tends to marry like is the general rule: marriages do not ordinarily occur between persons of different race, creed, or ethnic origin, nor between those widely separated in age, job, education, or social class." That is, outside of the movies, Harvard graduates from wealthy families do not often marry the daughters of impoverished Mississippi sharecroppers.)

Although our families are still nominally patrilineal since they take the surname of the father, in fact, family members accord no special reverence to the lineage of either parent.

Sons do not follow in father's footsteps, nor do they invariably heed father's advice. There are no rules that keep daughters within mother's kinship group. As young people go off to college, to jobs, to marriage, their ties to their families are progressively weakened; once they leave, sons and daughters in America rarely go home again.

To be sure, the younger generation and the older may retain considerable affection for each other, and parents may give material aid to help newlyweds get started, just as, later on, children may help out parents. But, in our society, emotional or material dependence on one's parents has come to seem a form of weakness. Today independence is highly valued. The individual's goals take precedence over the family's goal. One is expected to stand on one's own.

Whereas, in most of the societies we have discussed, there is a respected place for old people within the household, our society makes no such provision. A century ago, couples tended to marry later, have more children, and die younger than they do today. That meant they would probably have at least a child or two with them for their entire married lives. Such is no longer the case. As parents age, sons and daughters may contribute to their support, but the old folks are not often invited to come live with their children. That is not altogether due to the shortage of space in today's houses and apartments. Equally important is the fear that having parents and in-laws move in with one's own family is likely to create oppressive tensions and strains around the house.

Thus, many people in this society find themselves in the dusk of their lives existing alone in public or private homes for the aged, separated from their children and grandchildren. There is simply no place for them in the small family group. (The situation is quite different in China, where the traditional family was based on a father-son relationship and filial piety was the supreme virtue. We read of children who in a fire would rescue their aged parent and leave their own children to perish.)

Because the nuclear family is so small and so isolated, the emotional ties of its handful of members may become much more intense than they might be in a larger group, where many relatives share in the family life. This, it has been suggested, can lead to an emotionally overheated atmosphere, unhealthy both for parents and for children. It makes the growing-up process more difficult for the children and more painful for the parents. When the inevitable break occurs and the young leave the home, it may bring unhappiness and various forms of psychological distress.

The contemporary family, cut off from older generations and from other relatives, is not as stable or long-lasting as the extended family we have discussed. It may be that romance is simply not as enduring a cement for a marriage as property and social connections. Divorce is common today, and such breakups are all the more shattering for young children because they cannot depend on grandparents or aunts and uncles to care for them, emotionally or materially. The cooperation of kin that was part of frontier life has practically disappeared. The kind of support that flowed naturally in the extended family is not a natural part of today's situation.

We have referred to societies where, in case of divorce, the father simply goes off and the mother and child remain behind with the mother's blood kin, secure in the knowledge that they will continue to be cared for. Not so in America today. Today a divorce usually means that the mother is left to raise her children as best she can. The former husband may help to support his former family and arrange to spend weekends with his children, but there is no substitute for his presence in the home; that void remains.

What all this means is that the small urban family stands virtually alone, both emotionally and economically. And because it is alone, it can be severely shaken or even destroyed by death, divorce, chronic illness, prolonged unemployment, or other accidents of life. When such things happen these days, the family, or its surviving members, may have to count not on their blood relations but on the impersonal agencies of government to help them through the crisis. Even at their best, such agencies are scarcely able to provide the warmth of a kinship group bound by blood ties and by powerful tradition.

*

The apparent weaknesses of the typical American family that we have been discussing may be thought of as the price we are paying for its valued qualities. We have tried to show in earlier chapters that families everywhere have been formed to reconcile human needs with the needs of specific conditions and societies. It is not easy to find in history a family arrangement that would be better suited to the society we now live in than the nuclear family.

To be sure, some of us may have objections to aspects of the society, and so we may be critical of any family structure that supports them—but such issues go beyond the scope of this book. The nuclear family, with all its imperfections, is a remarkable instrument for meeting the private emotional and economic needs of most people.

As one scholar has observed, "Sexual unions without economic cooperation are common, and there are relationships between men and women involving a division of labor without sexual gratification, *e.g.,* between brother and sister, master and maidservant, or employer and secretary, but marriage exists only when the economic and the sexual are united into one relationship, and this combination occurs only in marriage."

Particularly in a highly industrialized economy such as ours, where most people do not get much satisfaction from their jobs, the emotional satisfactions provided by family life become all the more precious. That may be one reason why the marriage rate is so high—nine out of ten Americans marry at some time in their lives. And although a quarter of all marriages end in divorce, most divorced people re-marry before too long. In other periods, people *had* to get married; today, apparently, most people *want* to get married.

In recent years, the nuclear family has been attacked by women's groups in particular for its alleged unfairness to wives, for keeping them saddled with housework and child care while husbands go out to make satisfying careers for themselves. Whatever the justice of such charges—and there is a great deal of justice to them—we have to keep in mind that the inequities that today's women may suffer have a long history; they were not invented in twentieth-century America. As for our own time and place, never have household burdens been less heavy, never have women had more leisure or opportunity to pursue outside interests. To be sure, there is plenty of room for improvement, but it is unreasonable to blame the nuclear family for centuries-old discrimination against women.

As a matter of fact, there has never been a more open, more democratic style of family life than the one that prevails in America today. In few past societies would we find major decisions being made jointly by husband and wife, as they commonly are here. In few societies would we find so much regard for the rights of children to develop free of harsh treatment and repression. (On the contrary, the contemporary mother and father are often charged with being overly indulgent to their offspring.) Rarely before have the desires of young people been permitted to play a primary or even exclusive part in the selection of a mate, and the effort to make romance a continuing part of marriage is a conspicuous (if sometimes desperate) part of family life today. As relations with kin become less important, the marriage relationship becomes all the more important; husbands and wives today depend on one another much more than they did in the extended family. (One can argue that one of the reasons the divorce rate is high today is that marriage is too important to its partners for them to settle for less than they feel they need or should have.)

Even with all the intrusions of government in today's world, the relationships of husband and wife, of parents and children remain relatively free from outside authority—and authority within the home is applied with a much lighter hand than in the past. In what other era has the individuality of each family member been so respected? In what other era has personal happiness been the overriding goal of family life?

Like most human institutions, the family as we know it today has its share of strengths and weaknesses. Can it be changed to enlarge its areas of strength and reduce its areas of weakness? Undoubtedly—but changes in the family, like changes in human nature itself, do not occur overnight, and experience teaches that they cannot be brought about by passing a law or printing a manifesto. Still, let's take a quick look at what the future may hold.

SEVEN

The American Family: Tomorrow

What will the family of tomorrow be like—assuming that it exists at all?

Well, we are not prophets, but no great gift of prophecy is needed to see that changes which are taking place all around us must have an impact on our family lives. Examples are easy to find.

The availability of an easy-to-use, highly effective, apparently safe, relatively inexpensive birth-control pill is making sexual relations easier for both married and unmarried people. An unmarried couple can have sex without marriage; a married couple can have sex without children. Birth-control organizations, such as Population Zero, are lending moral support to the idea of childless marriages. The connection that we found in so many societies between sex, children, and marriage is loosening. (In some states unmarried individuals are now permitted to adopt children; thus, it may soon be feasible not only to have marriages without children but to have children without marriage.)

More and more years of education and training are required to prepare young people to take their place in our increasingly technical world. Because of this, marriage at an early age has become more difficult and less desirable from a dollars-and-cents point of view.

The opening of new careers to women means that girls are likely to find inviting alternatives to marriage awaiting them after high school. It also means that after marriage more women (particularly in the upper middle class) will choose to keep their jobs and, in a sense, be part-time wives and mothers. This cannot fail to have its effects on the operations of the household and the relationships of its members.

Large-scale efforts by local, state, and federal officialdom to provide for the needs of infants, young children, and the aged represent a benign impingement by the government on an area once reserved to the family.

The evident decline of the influence of religious bodies on personal relations has removed one of the traditional supports of the family and is leaving individuals more on their own in shaping their lives and those of their children.

We could go on—and so, no doubt, could you: the alleviation of household drudgery, a movement toward early retirement, the unprecedented explicitness about sex, the ever-increasing mobility of American families, the anti-family sentiments of some women's liberationists, and so forth. The list is long and impressive.

A reasonable case can be made that such changes add up to this sort of a situation: Fewer people will be getting married in the years to come; they will be getting married later in life and quite a number will get divorced; those who marry will have fewer children; women and men will contribute more equally to the family income, leaving the housework and much of the child-raising to machines, to the state, and to less affluent citizens.

All this is likely—yet, for as far as we can safely look into the future, we see most Americans (along with most people in most parts of the world) continuing to marry, set up a home, and raise their young much as they do today. The nuclear family does not seem to be in danger of instant annihilation.

But aren't we overlooking the fact that the kinds of changes we have cited are occurring at a much more rapid pace than social changes in the past? Won't the family have to adapt to them more rapidly—if it can adapt at all? It has been suggested that the pace of change today is so fast that the family in its present form cannot keep up, that it is already obsolete for most practical purposes and will in time simply be shucked off.

We have our doubts about that. Yes, jobs change, neighborhoods change, the world changes, sometimes with bewildering speed, and it is certainly true that the family is no longer the mainstay of economic life that it once was. But what about the effects of these changes on human beings? Aren't the changes making many people search for and cling to places and possessions and communities that they can be reasonably sure will not be blown away tomorrow? Isn't the speed and bigness and impersonality of American society causing many of us to treasure all the more those few deep, long-term relationships that don't follow the time clock of technology but move to slower, more natural, more human rhythms? Perhaps the society's swift pace will actually strengthen rather than weaken people's need for a family group of their own, and so strengthen the institution of the family.

We find ourselves unable to put much stock in futurologists who envision such developments as women being artificially impregnated and eliminating the most basic of men's functions. It seems to us that those who advance or even champion such mechanical arrangements as real possibilities for human beings are so entranced by the technology of the future that they fail to heed the lessons of the past. They are, it seems to us, a bit too casual about dismissing deep-lying human needs. No doubt a woman can produce a baby through artificial insemination. No doubt she can then entrust said baby to a state institution where it will be raised by efficient hands. Whether many women, or men, will find satisfaction in this kind of life style is another matter.

That is not to say that the nuclear family is the only kind of group that can provide basic human satisfactions. A lot of publicity has lately been given to innovative forms of family life such as communes, where a dozen or several dozen individuals not all linked by blood may live together in a kind of tribal arrangement. Such a way of life seems to express a longing for the warmth of the old-style extended family. As a Columbia University dean put it, "Communes are a device to make up for some of the things lost now in family life."

One such group which has existed for several years in Chicago brought together eight adults between the ages of nineteen and thirty-one and nine small children. One of the women who helped form it explained: "We wanted to simplify our lives by sharing property, instead of each adult owning separate furniture and appliances, and to enrich our lives by including many people in a home." At the beginning, each family had its own quarters in the commune's building, but this changed: "The building became one large home. Unless a door is closed, we are free to wander anywhere in the home, and to take part in whatever activities are in progress."

In most stable communes, observers have found, people develop brother-sister relationships similar to those made in the Israeli *kibbutz*. A researcher at Stanford University reports: "As people get defined as a family, incest taboos develop." Sexual activities among unmarried members tend to become unsettling; there is a noticeable preference for dating persons outside the household.

Communes are by no means the only innovation in family life. We have heard a good deal about "open marriages," in which both partners are free to establish sexual relationships with outsiders. And then there are "contractual" marriages, in which a woman and a man sign up together for an agreed-upon time; when the set period expires, they decide whether they want to renew the contract. And so on. There are many ways in which people can arrange their lives together, either within or without marriage, and we see no reason why individuals cannot achieve a full and happy (or not so full, not so happy) existence in any of them. Certainly, a marriage license is no guarantee of happiness.

Yet, if we still restrain our cheers for every new-style relationship that crops up, it is because we are unable to ignore or discount the biological differences between women and men with which we started this book. It seems to us, quite simply, that as long as women continue to bear children they will for the most part want to raise them. Nor can we discount the powerful emotional needs that bring two individuals together and keep them together or send them searching for a new relationship which, they hope, may prove more enduring than the one that didn't work.

Increasing numbers of young women are today choosing to pursue careers outside the home as an alternative to married life. Good luck to them. And many other women, especially in the upper middle class, are seeking ways of reconciling their desire for a career with their responsibilities to their families. This trend may work out well for all concerned. The children of a family in which both parents have strong outside interests may grow up feeling less oppressed by the intense single-minded supervision to which many middle-class children are subject today. The young mother can draw comfort from the knowledge that when her children reach home-leaving age, she will still have reward-ing activities ahead of her.

Certainly, women who are compelled by circumstances to give up their lives to keeping house and raising children are being deprived of many other experiences and are threatened with an empty old age. Yet we have the feeling that women who put too much of their hopes for satisfaction in a career outside the home may be in for a disappointment—the kind of disappointment that many "successful" men have been experiencing in recent years. There are mighty few lines of work, it seems to us, that offer the emotional rewards of bringing up one's children, and we are not convinced that the husband who goes off to an office every weekday is necessarily living a fuller life than the wife who stays at home.

Now, we would be less than honest with our readers if we neglected to remind them that we have been married for going on a quarter of a century and we have two children. We confess that we are very much part of a nuclear family and our views are undoubtedly colored by our own experi-ences. We are under no illusion that ours is the best of all possible families, or that the nuclear family is the best of all arrangements for people seeking to make good lives to-gether. But as we look over this short review of the long his-tory of the family, we are struck by the endurance of the ties between women and men, between parents and children. It is difficult for us to conceive of a society where these powerful ties have lost their hold on the majority of people. If we must place a bet either on the futurologists with their impersonal impregnations or on the family with all its strengths and failings, we'll take the family.

S E L E C T E D

B I B L I O G R A P H Y

Books on the Primitive Family by Nineteenth-Century Authors

The Development of Marriage and Kinship, by C. Staniland Wake, 1889; edited by Rodney Needham. U. of Chicago Press, 1967.
    This work by an amateur anthropologist is a good example of the nineteenth-century contribution to studies of the family. The author's close attention to detail does not make for easy reading.

The Family: An Historical and Social Study, by Charles F. Thwing and Carrie F. B. Thwing. Lee & Shepard, 1887.
    An eminently readable book that focuses on the family's relationship to the church, to property, and to the social order.

The Primitive Family in Its Origin and Development, by C. N. Starcke. Appleton & Co., 1889.
    In addition to covering the basic material on the primitive family, this clearly written book conveys the moralistic spirit in which early writers on the family approached their subject.

Primitive Society, by Edwin Sidney Hartland. Methuen & Co., 1848.
    A clear treatment of the origins of descent systems. The author's strained efforts to fit the evidence into evolutionary theories, making judgments about "higher" and "lower" forms of family systems, are common to works of the period.

General Books on the Family

The American Family in the 20th Century, by John Sirjamaki. Harvard U. Press, 1964.

A short volume, designed to interpret the findings of social scientists to the ordinary reader. It covers such subjects as the European background of the American family, the adaptation to the New World, courtship customs, and the changing status of children.

The Family, by William J. Goode. Prentice-Hall, 1964.

In this short volume, a sociologist deals with such subjects as the biological basis of the family, legitimacy and illegitimacy, and consequent household arrangements.

The Family: An Introduction, by C. C. Harris. Praeger, 1969.

The author takes a sociological approach to the subject, placing the European and American family systems in the context of world family systems.

The Family: From Institution to Companionship, by Ernest W. Burgess and Harvey J. Locke. American Book Co., 1945.

Taking the thesis that the family is in a transitional stage from its former institutional character to its present reliance on such intangibles as affection, sympathy, and comradeship, the authors document the change and consider the resulting problems. At the end of each chapter are questions and exercises, as well as a bibliography.

The Family in Various Cultures, by Stuart A. Queen, Robert W. Habenstein, and John B. Adams. Lippincott, 1967.

This informative, interestingly written little book contains, among other things, several chapters on specific family types in their cultural settings, as well as a lucid history of the Western family.

Marriage and the Family, by Francis M. Nimkoff. Houghton Mifflin, 1947.

A long book, but very clearly written, with illuminating photographs, charts, and tables. The sections on the hunting and farming cultures and on the American colonial family are especially interesting.

A Modern Introduction to the Family, edited by Norman W. Bell and Ezra F. Vogel. Free Press, 1968.

This hefty anthology, basic for students of the family, ranges from essays on the universality of the nuclear family to more specialized pieces on the family and personality. Of particular relevance to Chapter 4 of our book are two essays by H. Kent Geiger, "The Fate of the Family in Soviet Russia, 1917–1944" and "Changing Political Attitudes in Totalitarian Regimes."

Outline of the Future of the Family, by Carle C. Zimmerman. Cambridge, Mass.: Phillips Book Store, 1947.

Intended as a supplement to the author's college course on the family, this outline is especially valuable for its reading lists and the material on the trustee family of the fifth to twelfth centuries.

The World of the Family, by Dorothy R. Blitsten. Random House, 1963.

A highly readable, "comparative study of family organizations in their social and cultural settings," from the "corporate family" in Confucian China to the "bilateral extended family" in Latin-Catholic Europe.

Specialized Readings

Centuries of Childhood, by Philippe Aries. Alfred A. Knopf, 1962.

An original work which traces the development of the modern idea of childhood from the medieval concept of the child as merely a small adult.

Family and the Community in the Kibbutz, by Yonina Talmon. Harvard U. Press, 1972.

Through the use of first-hand interviews and direct observation, these excellent essays raise provocative questions about the relationship between the Israeli family and the kibbutz.

The Family: Its Function and Destiny, edited by Ruth N. Anshen. Harper & Row, 1959.

This anthology contains difficult but enlightening material on such subjects as "Parent and Child in Primitive Mythology," "Authoritarianism and the Family," and "The Family in China: The Classical Form."

Kinship and Family Organization, edited by Bernard Farber. John Wiley & Sons, 1966.

An interesting though difficult book that deals with the effects of kinship patterns on the nuclear family.

Kinship and Marriage, by Robin Fox. Penguin, 1967.

An introduction to the anthropological study of kinship. Although the later chapters may be difficult for a young reader, the earlier sections, in particular the discussion of incest taboos, are valuable and accessible.

Life and Leisure in Ancient Rome, by J. P. V. D. Balsdon. McGraw-Hill, 1969.

This illustrated work contains a chapter on family life in Ancient Rome that is fascinating in the variety of its detail. Working with such everyday materials as graffiti, graveyard inscriptions, and account books, the author fills out our understanding of the life of ordinary Romans.

INDEX